D0246813

CO 093545

Dumfries and Galloway Libraries, Information and Archives

This item is to be returned on or before the last date
shown below.

EwT

0 5 FEB 2008 EW

1 9 JUN 2008 EW

15TH JUly

5 AUG 2008 EW

28 OCT 2008 EW

14 AUG 2009 EW

12/10/04

DUMFRIES AND
GALLOWAY LIBRARIES
WITHDRAWN

1 9 JAN 2012 EW

5 SEP 2013 EW

385.0942

Dumfries and Galloway
LIBRARIES
Information and Archives

Awarded for excellence in public service
Dumfries and Galloway
Libraries, Information and Archives

Central Support Unit: Catherine Street  Dumfries  DG1 1JB
tel: 01387 253820   fax: 01387 260294   e-mail: libs&i@dumgal.gov.uk

24 HOUR LOAN RENEWAL BY PHONE AT LO-CALL RATE - 0845 2748080
OR ON OUR WEBSITE - WWW.DUMGAL.GOV.UK/LIA

*'Steam Past' Books from Allen & Unwin*

THE LIMITED by O. S. Nock
THE BIRTH OF BRITISH RAIL by Michael R. Bonavia
STEAM'S INDIAN SUMMER by George Heiron & Eric Treacy
GRAVEYARD OF STEAM by Brian Handley
PRESERVED STEAM IN BRITAIN by Patrick B. Whitehouse
TRAVELLING BY TRAIN IN THE EDWARDIAN AGE by Philip Unwin
MEN OF THE GREAT WESTERN by Peter Grafton

EWART

# Men of the Great Western

H. G. Forsythe

1. Centred around a fine display of lower quadrant signals, the atmosphere of the GWR lingers on in this picture taken at Newton Abbot in the summer of 1959. With steam roaring from the safety valves, a BR 2–10–0, piloting a GWR 2–6–2T, prepares to tackle the steep South Devon banks.

# Men of the
# Great Western

Peter Grafton

London
**GEORGE ALLEN & UNWIN**
Boston         Sydney

First published in 1979

This book is copyright under the Berne Convention. All rights are
reserved. Apart from any fair dealing for the purpose of private
study, research, criticism or review, as permitted under the
Copyright Act, 1956, no part of this publication may be repro-
duced, stored in a retrieval system, or transmitted, in any form or
by any means, electronic, electrical, chemical, mechanical, optical,
photocopying, recording or otherwise, without the prior permis-
sion of the copyright owner. Enquiries should be sent to the publishers at the undermentioned address:

GEORGE ALLEN & UNWIN LTD
40 Museum Street, London WC1A 1LU


© George Allen & Unwin (Publishers) Ltd, 1979

**British Library Cataloguing in Publication Data**

Grafton, Peter
    Men of the Great Western.
    1. Great Western Railway (Great Britain) – History
    I. Title
    385'.092'2    HE3020.G8    78–41060


ISBN 0–04–385075–8

EWART

Picture research by Mike Esau

Book design by Diane Sawyer/Design Matters




Filmset in 11 on 12 point Imprint
and printed and bound in Great Britain
by W & J Mackay Limited, Chatham

*For Kate*
*as promised*

# Contents

Illustrations

## Acknowledgements

I am very grateful for the whole-hearted co-operation of the men who feature in the following pages. They have been patient, tolerant, very hospitable and, perhaps more important, sympathetic and interested.

My thanks must also go to Pat Whitehouse for suggesting that I was capable of doing the job; to Mike Esau for his skilful assistance with the picture research and the captions; to Ursula Waterman, adept at interpreting my longhand and equally adept at typing; and to my wife Sally, who manages to teach full time and cope with the demands of a house and a growing family, yet ensures that I have time, opportunity and conditions in which to write.

Three Counties,                                                        Peter Grafton
Paignton,
Devon.
December 1977

H. G. Forsythe

14

2. At the start of another shift, the driver of Castle class 5076, 'Gladiator', walks towards the locomotive at Reading shed in 1960.

# I
# The Drivers

Those of us who have a deep interest in and love of steam, particularly if our memories go back to childhood, have a mental picture of the archetypal engine driver. To me as a child, engine drivers were of two well defined types. The one was rotund, jovial and pipe-smoking, ever ready to lean out of the cab window for a chat, and who might say 'Want to come up?' And there you would be on a hot, steamy and oily Mount Olympus with Zeus himself explaining the hidden mysteries of his charge.

The other type was tall, spare, angular, ascetic and, mark this well, if he smoked, which was unlikely, he smoked cigarettes. He was silent and his very demeanour forbade communication. Here was Charon, about to convey his load of souls across a metallic Styx.

But childhood memories are coloured by time and the footplate men to whom I talked whilst researching were in fact as diverse as the locomotives on which they worked.

Ted Reed joined the GWR in May 1917 at Birkenhead Junction, which was at the time operated jointly with the LNWR. He had of course to start as a cleaner, doing seven 12-hour days (or nights) per week for a wage of 7s 6d (37½p). Wartime conditions and shortage of manpower meant that promotion was rapid and, in October 1917, cleaner Reed became passed cleaner Reed, in recognition of which the company gave him an overcoat, and back he went to the cleaning gang.

When firing jobs became available they were, initially at least, restricted to shunting duties on an 0–6–0 ST in and around the docks, and the newly qualified fireman had to avoid the dual hazards of setting fire to the goods sheds and killing the shunting horses! At times when pay differentials are uppermost in people's minds, it is interesting to note that in 1917 a cleaner who was a passed fireman was paid as such only when firing until he had recorded 313 firing turns. Having reached this magical figure, he was then put permanently on fireman's rate of pay and was awarded three days' annual paid holiday.

In due course Ted was firing full time and was out on the main line. Initially this consisted of firing on tightly scheduled commuter trains – known as 'soap trains' – in and out of Port Sunlight but he eventually graduated to the more important turns, both passenger and freight.

During the Second World War, Ted Reed was promoted to locomotive inspector. He was always keen on mutual improvement classes and devoted much of his time not only to attending them but also to lecturing. His career as an inspector was relatively short-lived, however. On nationalisation, Birkenhead depot was taken over by the London Midland Region of British Railways and such was his loyalty to the GWR that he requested a transfer to an all-GWR depot. Thus Inspector Reed of Birkenhead became Driver Reed of Oxford and set about the business of 'learning the road' from Oxford to Paddington and from Oxford to Hereford.

Herbie Mitchell has about him an air of resilience, an almost calm philosophical air that probably stems from having spent his working life doing something that he enjoyed and during the course of which he was made redundant three times.

He joined the GWR in 1917 as a cleaner at Newton Abbot but when he was due for promotion to fireman he was given the option of either going to South Wales or leaving the company. This rather oversimplifies the situation because when he went to Swindon to have his 'firing medical' he had no idea where he would be sent. On passing the medical and on being given his uniform he was directed to Llantrisant. Unfortunately, the vacancy had been filled. So here was the newly qualified

3. A driver booking on at Reading shed in 1960.

H. G. Forsythe

N. F. Preedy Collection

fireman with all his worldly possessions in a tin trunk, a one-way pass from Swindon and no job. The shed foreman at Llantrisant sent Herbie to Newport but he was not required there either. Someone found him digs for the night and, when the powers that be at Swindon were told of the position, it was decreed that Herbie should stay at Newport as a fireman and he was allocated to coal train shunting duties. All was well until the coal strike of 1922. This effectively closed Newport Dock Street depot and once again our hero found himself redundant.

He was next directed to Ebbw Junction where, waiting for him and several other men,

were 30,000 tons of coal that had to be loaded on to trucks and moved to various parts of the country in an attempt to keep essential services going during the miners' strike. The target figure for loading was one ten-ton truck per man per eight-hour shift.

'With practice,' relates Herbie, 'some of us could load our trucks in six hours and have a couple of hours off. But this didn't suit the management so they got hold of sixteen-tonners and allocated two men to a truck, with forty men in a gang.

'Well, we'd just about shifted that heap when the strike ended and it all had to be put back again.'

4. Star class 4058, 'Princess Augusta', has the ash sucked out of its smokebox at Old Oak Common in 1960.

5. Far from its home shed of Old Oak Common, one of Churchward's mixed traffic 2–8–0s, 4707, waits for the next turn of duty at Birkenhead shed in August 1955.

During this labour of Sisyphus, Herbie was still employed as a fireman by the GWR but the guaranteed week was reduced to three days. Thus, for shovelling ten tons of coal per day Herbie, who was on the fireman's basic rate of 9s 6d (47½p) per day, was paid 28s 6d (£1·42½) per week.

After the miners returned to work, Herbie was soon back firing and shortly afterwards he was able to do a job swap with a fireman at Newton Abbot who was anxious to work in South Wales.

Although these early experiences are not strictly footplate experiences, they do illustrate working, and to a certain extent social, conditions as they existed immediately after the First World War, conditions that would today be as unthinkable as they would be intolerable.

In 1937, Herbie Mitchell became a passed fireman and he became a driver in 1938, retir-ing – this time a redundancy with a golden handshake – in 1964.

Bob Tucker joined the GWR as a cleaner at Llantrisant in 1920. Although he is a native of Newton Abbot and was intent upon a railway career, the only opportunity that he had of joining the company was to leave home and go to South Wales in the hope that he would be able to transfer to Newton when a vacancy arose. After several moves around the system, including time at Barnstaple and Tyseley, he eventually came back to Newton Abbot and retired as a top link driver in 1966. When I arrived at his house to do my first interview with him I found him seated in his favourite

18

6. The atmosphere of a main-line shed on a winter night is evoked in this picture of a 2–6–2T and Hall class 4–6–0 at Reading in 1960.

7. '. . . silent all night long we slept' – the words from Robort Louis Stevenson's poem, 'The Iron Steed', come to mind in this picture of a 4300 class Mogul in Reading shed.

*H. G. Forsythe*

armchair surrounded by notebooks and diaries and, as I was to discover during the course of about six hours of tape recording, possessed of an alert mind and with recall that had only rarely to be confirmed by reference to his notebooks.

Gilbert Lambert is a big, jovial man whose zest for life belies his age. I was introduced to him four years ago by a very good friend of mine who owns a hotel in Paignton. Gilbert was leader-organiser of a group of senior citizens from Westbury spending a week's holiday in the hotel. He was wearing his GWR tie with the panache of a Chelsea Pensioner sporting campaign medals, and my friend wasted not a moment in inviting him to join us at the bar. The conversation turned to firing, and in no time at all Gilbert had recreated the footplate of a Castle, using bar stools to delineate the fire-box door and the tender-firing plate. Then, with a walking-stick for a shovel, he showed us how to fire a Castle through Savernake. Although he had then been retired for sixteen years and probably had not fired a Castle for double that length of time, the wrist action was still there. So indeed was the enthusiasm that typified Gilbert, especially when he was talking of the GWR. He had so obviously enjoyed his working life, not with an earnest dedication redo-

8. An exterior view of Reading shed shortly after nightfall in the winter of 1960.

*H. G. Forsythe*

9. Banked by 'U' class Mogul 31802, Castle 5099, 'Compton Castle' climbs southwards towards Evershot with a well-filled Cardiff–Weymouth excursion on 14 August 1960.

*S. C. N*

W. Philip Conolly

lent of missionary zeal but with sheer exuberance, that I taped a conversation with him. At the time I did not know what I would do with the material but I had a feeling, almost instinctive, that here was something worth having on tape.

Gilbert left the peace and tranquillity of his uncle's farm in rural Wiltshire and joined the GWR in 1912 as a cleaner at Swindon. His motivation was, he admitted, money but he so enjoyed railway life that he never considered returning to the family farm.

Shortly after the outbreak of the 1914–18 war Gilbert was called for an army medical.

'I went in to the doctor,' he relates, 'and he didn't even look at me. "GWR fireman are you?" says he. "Yes, sir," I replied. "Ah, well," he says, "you'll be all right – carry on." '

And not many weeks after that Gilbert was in the army and on his way to Egypt where he spent some time on the railway that Field Marshal Allenby built through the Sinai Peninsula.

Demobbed in 1919, Gilbert was soon back at Swindon and, as war service counted towards seniority, he was very quickly out on main-line passenger work.

10. 'Is he doing it right?'

# 2

# The Daily Round

But to return to Ted Reed. Having done his stint as a fireman he was promoted to driver in May 1929, and began working his way through the 'links'. The allocating of engine crews to specific turns of duty was done by the depot administrative staff and was, of course, based on seniority and experience. Crews were grouped together in 'links' and the prestigious and important trains were therefore worked by men of the correct calibre, at least in theory.

Just what was involved in a link is well illustrated by the Birkenhead number two link, *circa* 1930.

| | | |
|---|---|---|
| (1) | Double home turn | – Bordesley – book off at Tyseley |
| (2) | Single home turn | – Oswestry |
| (3) | Single home turn | – local coal |
| (4) | Double home turn | – Smithfield meat – book off at Wolverhampton |
| (5) | Double home turn | – Wolverhampton passenger |
| (6) | Single home turn | – Shrewsbury margarine train express goods |

Double home – or lodging – turns were never very popular but were accepted as part of the job. Each important railway centre would have its collection of 'digs' – it was not until after the war that hostels were provided in centres other than London – and like seaside landladies some of the railway landladies achieved quite a reputation. A group of drivers in the BR staff Association Club at Newton Abbot waxed very lyrical about one particular place that they had to use when working the 'Salop'. One of them said that he used to have to wrap his shirt around the pillow because the pillowcase was dirty and another reported that it was quite common to get into a warm bed. 'Ah,' said another, 'but I once went to those digs after a night turn and a dirty so-and-so from Newport had been in the bed and you could see his outline in coal dust on the bedding. And I'll tell you another thing,' he went on, 'many's the time I've woken up with a complete stranger alongside me.'

'What about Old Oak? Do you remember? Three beds in a room, five of us sharing 'em and if you were on a night turn you had to have the window shut to keep out the noise.'

But they were all very quick to point out that most landladies looked after them very well and some even kept a rota. Not only

would they know who was on which turn but would know individual likes and dislikes.

I asked Ted Reed to give a typical example of a double home turn and after some thought he quoted the 4.5 p.m. Birkenhead–Smithfield meat'. This particular train was important not only to the men who worked it but to the GWR. Forty-eight refrigerated vans loaded with meat left Birkenhead docks at 4.5 p.m. every weekday bound for Smithfield Market where they were due to arrive at 11 p.m. There was an absolute deadline of midnight and should the train arrive after that time the GWR was charged demurrage of $\frac{1}{4}$d per pound weight of meat. Thus every encouragement was given to the train's crew to keep to the point-to-point timings.

The Birkenhead crew worked it to Wolverhampton and it was, of course, always away 'right time'. Immediately facing it was a

1 in 99 gradient, somewhat daunting for a cold engine but very useful for the driver for getting the feel of the engine and train. Then with passenger train timings there was a brisk run to Shrewsbury where a stop was made for brake testing, train examination and water.

During that first part of the journey via Chester and Wrexham, Gresford bank had to be tackled. At the start of the gradient the regulator would be wide open and the cut-off at 18 per cent. This would be advanced gradually to about 45 per cent at the top of the bank. Thereafter, on the relatively easy road through Chirk and Gobowen, speeds of 70–75 mph were maintained.

12. The low evening sun shows the graceful lines of Chirk viaduct to advantage as a freight heads north hauled by a Standard class 5. A class 47 diesel passes on the other line.

Brian Morrison

D. E. Esau

11 (*left*). One of Collett's chunky 5600 class 0–6–2Ts pulls slowly up the gradient out of Wellington with a pick-up goods for Wolverhampton in August 1952.

25

Brian Morrison

David A. Anderson

From Shrewsbury to Wolverhampton two stiff gradients faced the engine – Upton Magna and the climb from Shifnal to Cosford – following which there was an easy run through Albrighton into Oxley sidings, Wolverhampton. Here the 43 came off the train, a Hall backed on and the train was on its way to Smithfield with the minimum of delay.

The Birkenhead men handed the 43xx over to a disposal crew and booked off duty at approximately 6.15 p.m. They spent the night in Wolverhampton, booking on again at 6.15 a.m. the following morning and working a slow coal back to Birkenhead. Thus, during that particular week, they worked three double home turns with the 4.5 p.m. meat, interspersed with leisurely runs back to Birkenhead and followed by a rest day.

The Birkenhead–Shrewsbury margarine train was similar to the 4.5 meat in that it was an express freight with a perishable load. It was, however, a single home turn, the crew returning from Shrewsbury with a Bristol–Birkenhead tobacco train. Waiting time at Shrewsbury was occupied with engine servicing and with a meal break.

'We had three links at Newton Abbot,' recalled Herbie Mitchell: 'number three link

13 (*top*). The five 3100 class 2–6–2Ts were rebuilt by Collett in 1938 from the Churchward 3150 class. Here 3102 shunts at Wolverhampton before leaving for Wrexham with a freight in July 1954.

14 (*right, above*). 'Come on, mate!' The driver of 6004, 'King George III', has just finished oiling round at Exeter St Davids before leaving for Paddington.

15 (*right, below*). The down 'Cornish Riviera Express', which the photographer says ran in five parts on that day, on Dainton bank in 1937, hauled by Bulldog 3383 and a King. The headlamps are painted red.

26

shunting, number two was banking and short goods trips and number one was the main-line jobs. Included in number one link were three double homes – the Salop, the Penzance and the Paddington. There were twelve sets of men in each link and there was always six of them on double homes. And, of course, I musn't forget the spare link. We used to do two weeks in the spare and that could mean anything from double homes to shed duties. As far as I can recall we had about sixty locos at Newton. We had at least five Kings and the rest were Castles, Halls and the like. But give me a King any day. Mind you, you had to be big enough to work 'em. Long arms were a great advantage, especially when you were firing 'em.'

A typical working week for Herbie Mitchell contrasts very well with that quoted for Ted Reed up in Birkenhead.

'We'd take the 1 p.m. off Hackney Yard,' said Herbie, 'and get to Penzance booking off at about 9 p.m. Then next day we'd work the up TPO [travelling post office]. Following day we'd work the 8.30 a.m. Bristol coal empties booking off at 3 p.m. – that was a decent job – and then book on at 2 a.m. for the Brum goods. We'd follow that with the 3.45 a.m. Bristol goods and follow that with the 10.55 p.m. Westbury. Then we'd have a rest day. Your double homes were the Penzance and the Bristol.'

The 12 noon Plymouth–Paddington was Bob Tucker's example of everyday passenger-train working. 'It came up from Penzance behind a Castle and a 49 – Kings weren't allowed over the Royal Albert at Saltash. We'd be waiting with a King from Laira and as the Castle and the 49 came off the train we'd drop on and the fireman would go down and couple up. I'd then open the ejector and

create the brake. A carriage and wagon examiner would be around just in case there were any leaks anywhere. Everything OK, so put her in full forward gear. The guard would then pass on information about the train – 360 tons was the maximum allowed between North Road and Newton Abbot – and a pilot engine would be standing by in case we were over the allowance and needed assistance over Hemerdon bank. On this occasion we're alright. We get the right away so it's full forward gear and first valve of the regulator.

'As the engine gets hold of the train you must prevent slipping at all costs – it plays havoc with the fire that your mate has spent a lot of time building up. You could always tell when she was going to slip – you'd get a sort of death shudder. Now, the driver must watch his train right out of the station and once clear of North Road you had a rising road to Mutley tunnel. It was always wet so you'd put some sand down. Through the tunnel, notch up a bit and then watch for the 35 mph speed slack over Laira Junction. Notch up again and by Tavistock you're back to 25 per cent cut-off. Get to Plympton and it's full regulator for the bank. Hemerdon distant – 45 per cent cut-off and the shovel hasn't been out of the fireman's hand since leaving North Road. Both injectors are on and the King is really eating coal.

'Once over Hemerdon bank, pull her back to 20 per cent and full regulator. Carnwood–Ivybridge–Brent is a good running road and there isn't much to worry about until you're through Marley tunnel. Then comes a long drop down Rattery to Totnes. The regulator is on the drift and the cut-off at 45 per cent. As you get to Tigley at the bottom of the bank there are some reverse curves and you haven't touched the brakes since Plymouth

16. A June 1957 view from the cab of 6000, 'King George V', as it emerges from the west end of Dainton tunnel. The photographer notes that the loco was working at nearly full regulator and 40 per cent cut off.

K. H. Leech

but now it's about 12.30 and lunch is being served behind you. The passengers won't thank you for soup in their laps so gentle braking is needed for the curves. Lose about 5 inches of vacuum and keep it at that until you're through the curves. Once through 'em, blow the brakes off gently and look out for Totnes distant. It was about 1,000 yards from Totnes box and if it was off you knew that you had seven sets of boards at clear, so you could run through at about 40. If the distant was against you in foggy weather it could be dodgy – we used to get some nasty fogs off the river.

'Then we'd have Dainton bank and the tunnel. It's 1 in 38 up and 1 in 37 down and it's essential that the water level in the boiler is correct – if you got a surge over the top there was always the possibility of uncovering the crown. 45 per cent cut-off and careful around Stoneycombe curves. Aller distant comes into sight and you're on the drift. Open her up through Newton Abbot at about 15–18 per cent cut-off. Then we had eight speed restrictions between Newton Abbot and Exeter – the tunnels and Exminster troughs. Have a dip and get ready for Exeter.'

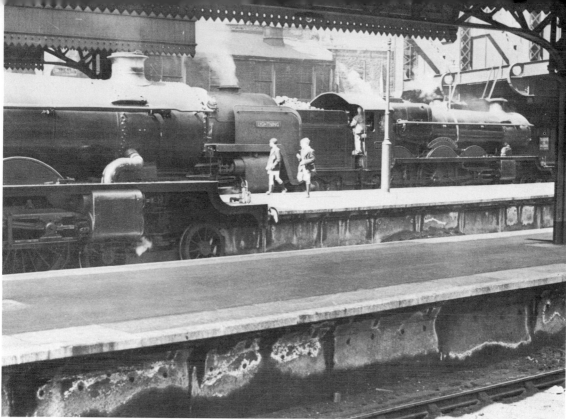

W. Philip Conolly

18. Three Saturday morning departures from Paddington – Britannia class 70019, 'Lightning', is caught between two Castles, 4074, 'Caldicot Castle', and 5004, 'Llanstephen Castle'.

When the mileage bonus was introduced, taking the place of bonuses based on oil and coal consumption, it was decided by consultation between unions and management that 120 miles was considered to be a day's work and additional mileage would be paid extra. Gilbert Lambert explained how this worked in practice:

'It was all right on the London,' he said. 'We'd be off Westbury at 8.40, arrive in Paddington at 10.15, run light to Old Oak, spend some time on checking the loco and have a spot of grub and then work the 12.30, into Westbury at 2.42 p.m., engine to shed, book off 3 p.m. Now we'd no prep. to do on that job

as we took over the engine so we'd booked on at 8.30 a.m. and done 197 miles on the round trip, 77 of 'em on bonus. But some jobs would fall just short of the 120 and then you had to see what could be done. We had one freight working to Weymouth and, especially in the potato season, we'd get off the train as quick as we could, turn her and hope that the shed foreman would be looking for a banker. "Got a spud – can you bank her as far as Bincombe?" "Yes we'll do it." You see, up to Bincombe and back took us over the 120 and put us on bonus. But they soon got wise and kept a banker at Weymouth.'

17 (left). Painted in the short-lived blue livery, 6026, 'King John', skirts the sea wall at Teignmouth with a train from Paddington.

Real Photographs Ltd

# 3

# Accidents and Adventures

Although it may not be appreciated, or even thought about, visiting the footplate of a stationary locomotive in steam is not without its dangers, particularly if the boiler is at or about its working pressure. The visitor or observer is almost surrounded by live steam and the failure of a gland or a gasket could turn a pleasurable experience into a tragedy. Consider then the potential dangers that faced footplate men every day of their working lives. Their trust and confidence had to be placed in designers, fitters, boilersmiths and boiler inspectors. Even then, the unexpected could and did happen. Gauge glasses might – and often did – break, or a steam pipe might fracture. But the footplate man's nightmare, which invariably happened without warning and was not always avoidable, was the blow back.

In 1945 I was having an unofficial footplate trip on an LMS 4–4–0 compound. We had just drifted through Barnsley Court House station and come to a halt at the up starter when without any warning an orange and black tongue of flame licked out of the firebox, completely filling the cab. I was deposited in a heap on the platform and suffered nothing more than hurt dignity. I was only twelve at the time but the incident is etched on my memory.

Ted Reed's blow back had far more serious consequences. It happened when he was firing a 2–4–0 T working a passenger train on the West Kirby branch.

'We were running bunker first and suddenly the blow back happened. It didn't last more than three seconds but during that time it burned most of the clothes off the right-hand side of my mate and the bunker plate was red hot. I was able to get right up against the cab side and I was all right but he couldn't – the lever rack was in the way. We got him to hospital but he was never right after that. He had a scar on his face that wouldn't heal properly and when he died it was reckoned to be the result of the blow back.

'It's difficult to say exactly what caused it but I reckon that he failed to open the ejector when he shut the regulator. Of course we were running bunker first and we might have had the dampers open.'

Herbert Mitchell told me that the blow back that he experienced was perhaps the most frightening thing that happened to him in a footplate career that spanned twenty-nine years. He was driving a Britannia class locomotive and was being piloted up Rattery bank.

32

19. 'I'm not joking: he must have been doing 95' —
conversation piece at Swindon Works in 1964 with the
frames of the now preserved Hall 4983, 'Albert Hall', in
the background.

'The Brit. was steaming well and we had the firehole doors open. As we hit the tunnel mouth, it happened – the cab was full of flames. We had the front dampers open and the blower was on but as the blower handle was somewhere in the middle of the flames, I couldn't get at it to open it up, nor could I get too far out of the cab because of the tunnel wall. Several things caused it: the pilot engine caused a change in pressure in the tunnel for a start and then the Britannias were very high and the top of the chimney was close to the tunnel roof. As I said, we had the fire-box doors open so all was set. I never went through a tunnel after that without making sure that the fire-box door was shut.'

Reference is made elsewhere and frequently to mutual improvement classes. The men of the GWR were enthusiastic about MI classes and acknowledged their value. One way in which the classes were used was to create theoretical situations and ask those attending to solve them, or indeed to use the classes to solve problems that had arisen. In this context Bob Tucker cited the case of the runaway engine, and here we had to consult his notes for the date – June 1937!

It seems that a 2–4–0 T engine, which had been on pilot duties in Newton Abbot station, was waiting to go back to Hackney Yard and by a singular coincidence was standing on a dead section of track – a section not track circuited. Under normal conditions, any locomotive would have bridged the dead section and completed the circuit, but the 2–4–0 T was physically too short to do this and was therefore unprotected: the signalman had no

indication of the engine's presence and, more important, the electrical interlocking of the signals was not operative. The signalman pulled off for a freight train on the through road and all was well set for a collision. The driver of the 2–4–0 T was vigilant enough to realise what was happening, put the engine into reverse and opened the regulator. But nothing happened. It was an engine equipped with slide valves and there was insufficient port opening to allow enough steam through to move the pistons – it was stuck on top dead centre. The 2–4–0 T refused to move and the driver and fireman followed Lady Macbeth's injunction and stood not upon the order of their going but went at once. The engine of the freight train hit the stationary 2–4–0 T and in so doing pushed the valves over the t.d.c. position. With the regulator wide open, off went the 2–4–0 T. Aller junction came and went, as did Kingskerswell, Torre and Torquay. Eventually, at Gas Works sidings between Torquay and Paignton, it ran out of steam and came off the track at a set of catch points having covered about eight miles.

According to the late Dr W. A. Tuplin, that iconoclast amongst railway writers, sticking on t.d.c. is impossible in a multi-cylindered steam engine, stationary or locomotive. My own footplate experience is indeed limited but a similar situation happened to me on a hot August afternoon in 1974. I was driving a three-cylindered piston-valve locomotive of somewhat larger proportions than Bob Tucker's 2–4–0 T and it resolutely refused to move when in full reverse gear and on the first valve of the regulator. It was only after several minutes' hard work – winding it from full reverse to full forward and back again that it eventually condescended to move. My apparent discomfiture provoked no end of hilarity amongst the platform enders and I was assailed with gems of wit. 'Has the spring broken?' 'Didn't know that you had to wind these things up.' Thus, when Bob was relating the incident, I was fully sympathetic.

Herbie Mitchell's blow back has already been related, and he recalled another, lighter incident which happened to him.

'I was working the 4 a.m. goods from Hackney – I can't remember what the loco was, probably a 28 – and we were checked at Teignmouth. My, it was a rough night – it was blowing and raining and we had the sea wall stretch to contend with. The board came off so away we goes. I looked out but we'd been stopped on a curved section of track and I couldn't see the lights of the brake van. I looked out several times and still couldn't see the van lights so I came to the conclusion that we'd left it behind. We got to Dawlish Box and I stopped to report it but the signalman knew – the Teignmouth man had seen us go by without the van. He'd got somebody to look for the van, and when they found it the guard hadn't even realised that he'd been left. What had happened, of course, was that the coupling had broken and as I said, it was such a bad night that the guard hadn't heard us go away. They then had to send an engine out from Newton and push the van after us.

If Herbie regarded the blow back as his most frightening footplate experience, he said that running it a close second was a burst tube.

'It was in the blackout, and we were banking, coupled, up Dainton with a 52 when a tube went at the fire-box end. Luckily, the fire-box door was closed so not much came into the cab. I got the blower on pretty quickly and checked the gauge glass. She had plenty of water in so obviously it wasn't a

20. In 1957 an immaculate Britannia 70028, 'Royal Star', is prepared at Ranelagh Bridge for its run back to Cardiff with 'The Red Dragon'.

plug. I shut off, of course, and used the brake whistle. The train engine driver reacted quickly and we were soon stopped. Me and my mate got off the engine and we shovelled ballast from the track on to the fire and put it out. Then we had to wait for a relief engine from Totnes.

'And talking of plugs, I did drop one – only once – but it wasn't my fault. After nationalisation we used to get foreign engines down here and I had a Midland engine on a pick-up goods from Newton to Taunton. We'd had a bit of injector trouble but what we didn't know was that we had a faulty gauge-glass as well. It was showing three parts full and as we got to Starcross – bang – she dropped a plug. Not much you can do except keep the doors closed and keep out of the way. Luckily we'd been turned inside on to the slow line so there we sat until they sent another loco out from Exeter and we were towed in.

'Of course gauge-glass breakages were commonplace. We always carried spares. Some would last for years but replacement was always tricky. You see, the gauge-glass frame would get twisted so that meant you might over-tighten the bottom nut and in so doing crack the glass. Then you might get scale from the water fouling the nut. I always carried a penknife and I'd give the nut and the seating a good scrape. Even so I've known three go, one after the other. And don't forget that if you were on the road you got no time allowance – you had to stick to your timings and replace the glass whilst you were still running. You imagine struggling to put in a gauge-glass whilst you're doing about seventy – every lurch of the engine twists the gauge-glass frame.

The injector is the means whereby water is moved from the tender tank, or the side tanks, into the boiler. Two types were usually fitted

21. 'You'll never do it that way.' Re-railing a GWR pannier tank at West Ruislip on 9 February 1952.

C. R. L. Coles

36

Hugh Ballantyne

– live steam and exhaust steam. The principle is quite simple – a jet of steam at high pressure is forced through a cone and in so doing its pressure is increased. If water is allowed to come into contact with the steam it will pull the water with it.

The plug mentioned in the same incident is a safety device. The water level in the boiler must always be above the top – or crown – of the fire-box and fitted in the crown are fusible plugs. These are similar to the washout plugs that can be seen on a boiler and fire-box except that they have lead core. If the fire-box is uncovered – if the water level drops – then the temperature will increase and the lead core in the fusible plugs will melt. The result is that steam is forced through the centres of the plugs into the fire-box with the object of extinguishing the fire. But the steam is at normal boiler pressure and the effect of jets of steam on the fire is to blow it out of the fire-box door – a dangerous procedure. Of all the symptoms of ineptitude and mismanagement, that which is considered by enginemen to be the most unforgivable – or least excusable – is dropping a plug.

22. A Churchward 2800 class 2–8–0, injector on, toils up the east side of Dainton bank assisted at the rear by a 2–6–2T.

Bob Tucker, talking about Exminster, said:

'I was working a freight from Newton Abbot to Taunton with a 28xx class loco and when me and my mate took it over we checked that the indicator on the tender showed plenty of water. As we had a very light load, particularly for a 28, I told him not to bother having a dip at Exminster. Just approaching Cullompton the injectors flew off. My fireman went on to the tender and had a look in the tank – no water. We blackened the fire straight away and as we approached Tiverton I sounded the whistle. The signalman very quickly got the message and just as quickly we had the water crane bag into the tender. It seemed to be an age before the injectors picked up. We both learnt a lesson – don't trust the tender float and always have a dip at the troughs. But at least we saved the plug.'

37

# 4

# Rules and Regulations

The GWR maintained discipline amongst its operating staff by being almost paternalistic, and the company had a safety record of which it was, with some justification, very proud. When a fireman became passed to drive he had, of course, to be familiar with the routes over which he was to work. He may well have worked them as a fireman but still had to sign the route book indicating his familiarity with a particular 'road'. Now a driver who was 'learning the road' was rostered to it either as a spare driver or as a fireman and he devoted as much time to it as he himself felt to be necessary. He was not pressured by locomotive inspectors or by management and when he felt competent he would 'sign for the road'. Having done so he was thereafter totally responsible and, whilst the company was quite willing to let a driver take his time, once he had committed himself his knowledge of the route was gauged from his timekeeping whilst driving over it.

Point-to-point timings were very important. A variation of a minute either way from the working timetable was noted and anything in excess of five minutes was subjected to an inquiry. If the delay was shown to be due to circumstances beyond the driver's control then there was no further action taken but if a driver was at fault then there were several disciplinary procedures from which to choose. (This, of course, also applied to offences other than poor timekeeping.) A verbal caution might be issued – this would probably be a rebuke from the depot foreman to the effect that 'you've been a naughty boy – watch it in future'. More serious offences might warrant a registered caution in which case the unfortunate recipient would be interviewed by a locomotive inspector and the incident noted in his records. Three of these meant automatic dismissal. Very serious offences – gross negligence, drunkenness on duty – would bring immediate suspension followed by a full-scale inquiry. It is worth noting here that one of the country's first railway strikes was precipitated by the dismissal of a driver who was fined for being drunk and disorderly some thirty hours before he was due to report for duty. That was thought to be carrying things too far, and the company concerned was not the GWR.

Ted Reed was rostered to an express passenger from Oxford as a spare driver and he spent some time getting the feel of the route. Coming through the Thames Valley one day, he took over the regulator of the Castle and all

went well as far as Paddington. Now there was a 5 mph speed restriction into Paddington and driver Reed passed the end of the platform at about 25 mph. He relates that there was consternation all round as the Castle headed for the buffers but all was well and he brought his train to a halt with little trouble. He says that he was blissfully unaware of the speed restriction but that the platform inspector at Paddington left him in no doubt whatsoever! He records that he did eighty trips between Oxford and Paddington before he signed for the route.

Another illustration of the importance of the rules is what happened when Bob Tucker was working a Newton Abbot to Plymouth freight with a 28xx loco.

'We were stopped and the signalman told us that he'd seen a herd of cattle charging into the down side – our side – of Marley tunnel. Now Marley is a split tunnel – it has a curtain

23. The down 'Cornishman' ascends Rattery bank during the transitional period between steam and diesel traction, hauled by a Warship diesel D831, 'Monarch' and Hall 6946, 'Heatherden Hall'.

wall separating the up and the down sides. What to do? Well, I sent my mate on to the buffer beam with a flare lamp and then went very cautiously through the tunnel. Couldn't see any sign of the cattle – we reckon that when they got out of the other end they scrambled up the bank. You see, we applied the same rule that governs the first train through any tunnel after the permanent way people have had possession – even though you're told it's clear the first train through must proceed at caution just in case any equipment and so on has been left inside. Once that train is through and all is OK then the driver informs the signalman whose section includes the tunnel and then and only then do you get back to normal working.'

Bob used to devote much of his spare time

39

to lecturing to mutual improvement classes and he specialised in rules. Once he anticipated in theory in the classroom an incident which actually happened a few days later. It was just at the time when diesels were being introduced, and a Warship class diesel was working a partially fitted freight train over Dainton bank, assisted in the rear by a 63xx loco. About half-way up the bank the diesel stopped without any warning – the inexperienced driver had lost his deadman, the device that completely shuts down everything on the diesel locomotive if it is released – but the 63xx carried on pushing for a time before the driver realised there was anything amiss. Both firemen acted correctly: they left their respective engines, protected the other road with detonators and then met and examined their train. They found that the 63xx had pushed one of the loose-coupled wagons over one of the vacuum-braked wagons. Fortunately,

there was no obstruction to the other line and the travelling post office, the next train due in the opposite direction, was able to pass at reduced speed.

Although the drivers to whom I talked had worked on different sections of the GWR on different types of locomotives, and each had developed his own technique, they were agreed on one fundamental part of the footplate man's job – engine preparation and particularly that aspect of it that was the fireman's responsibility. The routine procedures that were carried out during the time that was allocated were essential not only to the efficient operation of the locomotive but to the forming and moulding of the individual's attitude to his job. It should be remembered that whilst promotion through the grades from cleaner to fireman, from fireman to junior driver and eventually to top link driver

D. A. Anderson

H. G. Forsythe

24 (*above*). The fireman of 4074, 'Caldicot Castle', takes a breather as the loco accelerates past Didcot in 1960.

25 (*right*). The primitive conditions with which staff had to contend in the steam era are shown in this picture of a fireman tidying up the front end of Worcester Modified Hall 6989, 'Wightwick Hall', at Reading shed.

*Photomatic*

26.  Spot the locos – Swindon 'A' shop in 1932.

was progressive it was not necessarily automatic. The training that a man received was essentially practical and, although mutual improvement classes were organised by the company, attendance was voluntary and any such in-service training was not given in the company's time. Bob Tucker told me how he used to go straight from a heavy eight-hour shift to an MI class or, if he was on night shift, leave home a couple of hours earlier than usual and go to work after having attended a class. Not unnaturally, the company was aware of the men who were prepared to give up their time to attend the lectures.

The classes consisted of study sessions on rules and regulations and the consideration of how to deal with given circumstances should they arise, or indeed had they arisen. A very good illustration of this occurred when Castle class locomotive 4016 failed whilst hauling the 'North Mail' and coming through Dawlish knocked out the left-hand inside cylinder cover. The crew managed to bring the engine and train into Newton Abbot and the train continued its journey with another engine. Meanwhile, 4016 was moved into the shed, which, according to eyewitnesses, almost disappeared in clouds of steam, and Swindon was notified of the incident. Back came a message to the effect that 4016 must not be repaired at Newton Abbot as the Chief Mechanical Engineer's department was anxious to investigate the cause of the failure — 4016 must be returned to Swindon under its own steam. Now this posed quite a problem as the valve gear for the outside cylinders of a Castle derive their motion from rocking levers actuated by the inside cylinders, but a solution had to be found and the case history was presented to a mutual improvement class at Newton Abbot by a locomotive inspector. The answer to the problem was to remove the pistons from the inside cylinders, leaving the cross-heads in position: the inside valves had to be centred to prevent loss of steam from the inside cylinders but it was then found that in this position the inside radius rods fouled the valve spindles. Then someone — we know not who — came up with the bright idea of reversing the valves so that the spindles protruded from beneath the smokebox. And in that condition 4016 ran light engine to Swindon on two outside cylinders.

# 5

# The Great Western at War

'The Great Western at War' – just what image does that conjure in the minds of those who have no recollections of 1935–45? Many films have been made spotlighting the work and efforts of the services, but no one took the trouble to take a camera and crew into a blacked-out depot or into the sheeted cab of a locomotive. No film record of a night-shift fitter trying to carry out effective maintenance with the minimum of light and without a mate – he'd joined up; no record of the driver and fireman struggling to keep a poorly maintained engine steaming on sub-standard coal, pulling a load far in excess of that for which it was designed on track that was years overdue for relaying. But let Herbie Mitchell take up the story.

'Conditions in general were bad during the war. When I started firing they'd stopped the one engine, one crew arrangement but they were still allocating shed days for crews to do boiler washouts. The one engine, one crew was stopped when the working day was reduced to eight hours. They got more work out of an engine by allocating it to different crews but, even so, steam locos never became common user locos in the same way as diesels. You see, when the phasing out started at Newton we lost a lot of goods traffic and we lost some of the double homes including the Salop job – this was always a Newton Abbot job but it was split between Newton men and Shrewsbury men – we'd take it to Bristol and they'd take it on but the loco was always returned to its home depot.'

Wartime provided Bob Tucker with one or two nasty moments, not necessarily connected with enemy action.

'One night,' he said, 'I was standing at Taunton with a 28xx class on a slow freight to Exeter. We were usually put inside there to let the 9.55 p.m. Bristol fast freight get in front of us. On this particular night, the 49xx class engine on the fast freight dropped some firebars. They commandeered my loco and told me to work the faulty 49 to Exeter. I had a look at her and I could see that the ashpan was full of fire. I got on to control and said that I wouldn't move until they could guarantee me a straight run through with no signal checks. When they asked why, I told them that included in my train were half a dozen petrol tankers – full – and I didn't like the idea of them standing at a signal above some fire that I might have dropped. I got straight through all right but it wasn't one of my most pleasant experiences.

'Of course you have to realise that during the war, certainly in the early days, the loco cabs were blacked out. They had a tarpaulin stretching from the roof half-way along the tender and side sheets covering the cab windows – working conditions weren't so good, particularly on warm nights. One of my mates was rostered to the midnight from Newton Abbot to Paddington. As usual it was packed to capacity, mostly with servicemen, and she came in from Plymouth behind a Castle. A King took over at Newton and the fireman went down to couple up. Whilst he was doing this two soldiers climbed up on the tender – they hadn't any money for the fare to Exeter – and when the fireman was back up, off she went. Now for security reasons we weren't allowed to fire along the sea wall so once you were off Teignmouth there wasn't much for the fireman to do until Exminster troughs. You always had a dip there – it was essential coming down and a bit of an insurance going up. The troughs were 560 yds long and the maximum speed to ensure a good dip was about 50 mph. There was quite an art in taking water at speed. If you got your scoop down too soon you stood a good chance of damaging it on the end of the trough: if you didn't get it down soon enough you'd only get half a tank full: if you didn't get it up in time you'd have water and coal all over the footplate and if you had it in too deep you had no chance of getting it up until the end of the trough and you'd probably wash your coal down anyway.

'Well, my mate's fireman has a dip at Exminster and he overdid it. Before leaving Newton he'd been careful to put on as much coal as he could with due regard to safety because he knew that he had a heavy train and that signal checks were almost a certainty. He didn't get the scoop out in time and sure enough, the cab's flooded. A lot of his coal comes down, and with it two pairs of boots. The driver stopped the train and then the two of them pulls two wet, dirty and frightened men on to the footplate. It was impossible to tell whether they were English or Germans but having sorted that out the train carried on to Exeter and these two fellows shot off down that platform and disappeared. The driver reported it and, as a result, all engines on night passenger trains were examined for unofficial passengers before leaving Newton.'

Going back to Herbie Mitchell, he recalled that there were a lot of troops, especially Americans, in the Newton Abbot area. 'The last trains, particularly on Saturdays, could be crammed. I've seen Paignton station so crowded you wouldn't believe it. I worked a King on a train down to Kingswear one night and the rostered job was to leave the coaches, turn the engine at Kingswear and then light engine to Newton, the guard riding with us. On this occasion I decided to run back tender first. There was a lot of overcrowding at Newton – they had more locos in than they could handle and if you didn't get back and get on one of the shed roads you could be hanging about waiting for a place or even doing some shunting. So, off we goes. Of course, the cab was all blacked out with side sheets and tarpaulins, and as we approached Britannia crossing I put my head out and whistled.

'As we went through the gates I saw a light falling past the tender. I was doing about 25 so I pulled up and sent my mate and guard back to have a look. They came back and said they hadn't found anything and reckoned I'd seen a shooting star. Now from Kingswear station as far as Britannia there was a footpath alongside the line and I was always worried about the servicemen walking along the line in the blackout. You should have seen 'em sometimes in Kingswear station when they'd had a few – insist on staggering along the platform or across the track to say goodnight to the driver. So I got off the engine and we all three went back and I found a serviceman's cap and a torch by the side of the track – it was the torch that I'd seen falling by the tender. "There's your shooting star," I said to the guard. And then we heard the moaning, coming from over the wall by the side of the track.

As you know, the river embankment comes right up to the side of the track. We climbed on to the wall and using the guard's lamp we eventually found a soldier on his back in the mud and in a bad way. I went to the crossing keeper's cottage and there was a couple of American soldiers in there. One of 'em went up to the camp by Phillip's yard and the other came back with me. We didn't want to move the injured man but as the tide was coming in we hadn't much choice. You have to hand it to

the Yanks, they had things organised. They soon had a rescue boat with searchlights on the job and the medical officer from the camp came down and examined the man and sent him to Brixham hospital. After that we carried on to Newton. There was an inquiry, of course, and there was disagreement about the man's injuries. One doctor said that he was hurt jumping over the wall and another said that he'd been hit by the corner of the tender and knocked over the wall. But in any case he was trespassing. Anyway, it's not everybody who has been knocked down by a King and survived.'

Another exciting wartime incident occurred when Bob Tucker was working a heavy train of scrap metal from Devonport Dockyard to Westbury. Bob and his mate took it over at Newton Abbot and all went well as far as Whiteball.

'She was steaming well,' said Bob, 'and as we approached the tunnel I found that the vacuum brakes weren't working – there was a defect on the reservoir side and the cross-head pump was actually pumping the brakes off.

We screwed down the hand brake as hard as we could but of course we had a trainload of cut-up ships and that sort of thing and away we went. Well, the distant at Wellington was against us and so I began to blow the brake whistle – GWR engines were fitted with two whistles, one for normal use and the other called the brake whistle, used for whistling for brakes or in emergencies – and ran past the outer and inner home signals and the starter. We got to a stop just before the advanced starter. This meant that the signalman didn't have to send 'train running away on right line' signal to the next box but he did get on to Taunton and arrange to have the loco examined. We got to Taunton but the fitters couldn't do much so we went very slowly to Westbury, let the fire down and reported it as defective. About three weeks later me and my mate booked off at Bristol and as we walked through the shed I spotted the same 28 class tucked away in a corner with its front end stove in. A quick repair job hadn't been very effective – wartime, you know – and somebody had been less lucky than us.'

27. Shortage of materials and security meant that amateur photography was almost impossible during World War II, and official photographs of the period are fairly few in number. This picture is of a coal train at Severn Tunnel junction in September 1942.

British Rail

# 6

# The Kings

The Kings, introduced by Collett in 1927 at the behest of Sir Felix Pole, were to the GWR what the A4s were to the LNER, the Stanier Pacifics to the LMS and the Lord Nelsons to the Southern. This is hardly the place to argue the merits and demerits of the Kings as a class: one thing which is certain is that they were held in great affection by the men who worked on them.

'A King,' said Herbie Mitchell, 'would do anything that was asked of it provided that it was well maintained. In the war I've worked Kingswear–Newton Abbot–Paddington with sixteen on – no problem at all. Mind you, your fireman knew that he'd been to work. And you could only do that sort of work if you had coal in the tender. We used to get all sorts. Not only was there poor coal but we had ovoids, briquettes and even coke at one time. Firing a King with briquettes was like giving a donkey strawberries, and as for coke, well, you'd be stopping to blow up every so often. I've gone from Newton to Westbury many a time and every loop has been occupied. It was bad enough not having the line capacity for the traffic that we had to handle in the war but then when you were having to go inside to the slow line to clean the fire and get enough steam to crawl to the next loop it could be a nightmare.

'To give you some idea, I mentioned a good run with sixteen on, well, I came back from Paddington with a King with sixteen on. It was a Christmas during the war and she was loaded right up. We were supposed to be first stop Torquay and we left with a tender full of good stuff for a change but by the time we reached Torquay there was about a hundred-weight left. We'd had so many stops and starts that she'd used about five tons of coal. You think about it – the best part of 500 tons behind the tender takes some moving from a dead stop. The other thing that used to worry me when the coal got a bit low was when we came to the water troughs – the tender lifted on its springs and the scoop would barely skim the surface.'

As will have already become clear, Bob Tucker had a particular interest in rules and regulations, especially those introduced for the protection of disabled trains. But, as Bob said, rules can sometimes be broken quite unwittingly.

'I was working the Kingsbridge branch with a 45xx tank engine and was instructed to return to Newton light engine but this was in the early part of the war, traffic was heavy and

48

28.  The fireman's view from 6000, 'King George V', on the westbound 'Cornish Riviera Express' dropping down to Totnes in June 1957.

there was no path for us. We hung about for ages at Brent and then the signalman came over and told us that our only chance of getting back was to pilot the up parcels so we crossed over as soon as he arrived. Now, it is the duty of the train engine crew to attach a pilot engine and the duty of the pilot crew to detach. Well, the train engine fireman did his job, we got there right away and got to Newton without much bother. I had a very young fireman at the time and I decided that I'd uncouple because we were in a hurry, it was dark, it was the blackout and the only light that we had was the gauge glass lamp. I wanted to be sure that the vacuum pipe on the train engine was on properly – otherwise we'd have been delayed at Newton. I got down and as I was uncoupling I was struck by the size of the train engine. I had another look and then realised that we'd piloted a King over Dainton. I got my loco out of the way and on to the shed as quickly as I could. You see, the rules specifically banned the piloting of Kings by

29. Some passengers are clearly interested in the reasons for the slow running and delay – blue-liveried 6012, 'King Edward VI', is working cautiously on the wrong line at Southcote junction during engineering works in 1951.

30. With a less than tight front end, a King accelerates out of Reading with the down 'Cornish Riviera Express' in 1955.

D. Hepburn-Scott

M. W. Earley

anything less than a four-coupled bogie engine – with anything smaller there's always the danger that the pilot engine might be pushed off the road. As far as I know that was the only time that it happened and the management was none the wiser.

'Another time, I was working a semi-fast from Newton to Plymouth with a King, and as we approached Ivybridge station I eased her for the 40 mph restriction. My mate and I were both sitting down when there was suddenly a lurch and I thought that we were off the road. If we'd been standing up I reckon that we'd both have been injured. Anyway, I

looked out, saw that a permanent way gang was at work, got a wave from the chargeman and carried on. But the train following us wasn't quite so lucky. It was the 'Cornish Riviera' carrying heads of the armed forces, going to Plymouth for a conference. The King became derailed, or at least the bogie came off going through Ivybridge. It ran through the station, smashing all the chairs as it went, and then it re-railed itself on a set of points at the end of the platform. It sheared thirty rivets on the suspension bar and the driver said afterwards that he stopped because he thought that he was having a

51

H. G. Forsythe

rough ride. He got down to inspect and was surprised to find that a length of rail was missing. Well, he notified control, inspected his engine, decided that it was safe to proceed and at a reduced speed brought the train into Plymouth. That shows how superbly the Kings rode, and how a permanent way error of only a couple of inches could and almost did cause a serious accident.'

The highlight of Gilbert Lambert's footplate career came, he maintained, when he was rostered to a special that was to test the alignment of an avoiding line that had been laid from Heywood Junction to Fairwood, thus bypassing Westbury.

The train consisted of eight coaches and the GWR dynamometer car hauled by a King class 6022, 'King Edward III', and amongst the somewhat exclusive passenger complement was C. B. Collett, then Chief Mechanical Engineer of the GWR. Gilbert's instructions were clear and unequivocal – 90 mph between Eddington Junction and Whitham. So, with two of Collett's technical assistants

31. An unidentified King receives attention to its inside cylinders in Old Oak Common shed.

on the footplate, the train set off and reached the prescribed 90 mph before braking for Whitham. Here the engine came off the train and ran round the triangle, and the instructions for the return journey were even more unequivocal than those for the outward run – as fast as you can over all the junctions, a clear road guaranteed to Bratton. One of Collett's assistants asked Gilbert how he felt about it and received the answer, 'Look here, if I go out into the bloody fields, you've got to come with me.'

'Well,' said Gilbert, 'we got away from Whitham and the clock went round to 100 and she stuck there and the only place that the King's nose wanted to go out into the fields was at Heywood. I slammed down after we got off the junction – I had kept her going over the junction and when I shut off she hung on at 100 for some time. Anyway, everybody seemed quite pleased.'

52

# 7

# The Team

There is no doubt that rapport between driver and fireman was absolutely vital so far as preparation and working together was concerned. What was more, in the days of double home turns, when men had overnight stops, driver and fireman shared not only the same lodgings but often the same bed.

When two men work and live so closely clashes are almost inevitable, although it seems that serious disagreements were rare. Arguments and squabbles that did take place on the footplate seemed to stem from the fireman accusing the driver of working the engine too hard! On the other hand, the driver might be saddled with a lazy fireman. In any event, a driver could have the last word when it came to the promotion of a fireman.

Gilbert Lambert spoke about the driver with whom he worked for fourteen years.

'He was the type of driver who expected the fireman to do all the preparation and who was obsessed with time. In fact he was known as the heaviest driver at Westbury. We'd leave Paddington and he'd be on full regulator to Reading and I had my head in the fire-box all the way. If I complained he'd say "Well, my son, we now got plenty in hand." He never had a late report and we'd run into Westbury well before time with the smokebox ashes above the blast-pipe. I'd then go home and have to change all my clothes – soaked to the skin. I once threatened to make an official complaint but all I got was "Don't forget that I can sprag you, my son, when you goes up to Swindon for driving."

'I was transferred temporarily to another link and my mate there was just the opposite. I'd come home from work and do a spot of gardening – the wife couldn't understand it.

'The only serious disagreement that I had with my regular mate was when 3814 was reported for poor steaming – he'd reported it, mind. We went off the shed and on to our train and we were joined by an inspector. He said to me, "Get up in that seat – I'll do the firing", and he did from Westbury to Reading. I finished off the trip to Paddington and I'd been watching that driver – he'd worked the engine different to his usual style. Anyway, I was annoyed so I didn't clean the fire while we was at Old Oak. I thought no, let the inspector do it. But he didn't. He came on with us and said he was only going to Reading and I had to fire. He got off and said that he'd check with us next day. The engine hadn't steamed at all badly and no wonder. He'd been at 45 per cent cut-off most of the way and only on the first valve.

S. C. Nash

'Well, we set off next day and he was up to his old trick – I'd tumbled to it by now. He'd open the regulator to the second valve and then move the handle back gently. You see then it would look to the fireman as though the regulator was only on the first valve. We had much heavier coal consumption and when we got to Reading I dropped off the footplate and said, "I'm going to look for that inspector – we've used more coal coming to Reading than we did to Paddington yesterday!" "Don't be too hasty," he says, "see what we does going back." He wasn't too bad going back but at Savernake I had to go across to him and shut the regulator. "Twenty-seven miles downhill," I said to him, "no need for that bloody thing on the second valve." And after that we didn't have a wrong word.'

The official meal break would see a flurry of activity. The shovel would be washed clean with the slacker pipe and wiped with a piece of cotton waste. Driver – or fireman – would be cook and the contents of their food boxes – bacon, sausages, potatoes and egg – would be garnished with mushrooms and fried over the fire. The food would be eaten from tin plates that had been warming on the shelf above the fire-box door and be washed down with tea made in the signal-box. 'Eaten in the crisp morning air,' said one former driver, 'it was a feast that would make any gourmet drool with delight.' Unfortunately, the Company, not unreasonably, discouraged the use of the fireman's shovel as a frying-pan as it took the tempering out of the steel and thus shortened its useful life, so the enterprising driver or

32 (*left*). Teamwork at Savernake – a pannier tank tops up with water before working a train to Marlborough.

33. The cars in the station forecourt and the advertisements give a clue to the date of the picture. Castle 4087, 'Cardigan Castle', has arrived at Torquay with the 1.25 pm Paddington–Kingswear whilst 2–6–2T 5558 is station pilot. The date? 14 June 1958.

John Ashman FRPS

fireman would ferret around the shed and retrieve a discarded shovel from the scrap heap. It would be cleaned and burnished and kept specifically for use as a frying-pan. Foot-plate clashes sometimes occurred, for example when a driver, pulling rank, insisted on frying his kippers before his mate fried his bacon and sausages. When the fireman pointed out that sausages tainted with the flavour of kippers are not very palatable, the driver conceded, but he accidentally caught the blower handle just as the sausages and bacon were cooked to perfection and they disappeared into the maw of the fire-box. There is, alas, no record of the conversation that ensued.

Steam locomotive firemen are not easy to find – there are not many of them about. The reason for this elusiveness is not difficult to explain. Whilst I had few problems in contacting retired drivers, I failed to locate a retired fireman because firemen invariably became drivers before they retired. Admittedly, several of the drivers to whom I spoke introduced

reminiscences of their firing days but I was looking for the genuine article – someone who had been a fireman and only a fireman during all his working career. Now this presented me with the problem that the title of this book includes those magic words, 'Great Western', not 'Western Region'. But principles are all very well if one can afford them and in the end I had to settle for a former Western Region fireman who was made redundant after eighteen years' service. John Twitchen is now a post office engineer and nine years after having left railway service still admits to missing the life. He joined BR at Exeter in 1950 as an examiner's mate but his ambition was to get on the footplate. He subsequently became a cleaner and had to move to Old Oak to become a fireman. Following national service in 1955 he came back to Exeter as a fireman.

'Although firing one big engine was very much like firing another,' said John, 'you obviously had to have different techniques for different classes. The Kings and Castles had twelve-foot long fire-boxes with sloping grates. You'd always fill up your back cor-

34 (top). On 9 October 1951 the crew of Collett 0–6–0 3202 and the shunter pause for their picture to be taken in Minford yard. The loco is painted in green livery and, despite its British Railways smokebox numberplate, has what appears to be a Dean tender, lettered 'GWR'.

ners, build your fire well up under the fire-box door and then slope it away towards the front, and then of course always fire to the brightest part – no good putting coal on a black fire. The technique with the tank engines that we used on the valley lines was different – keep your fire saucer-shaped with all corners filled except with the 45s – they had mini-King fire-boxes. We had some fun when we began to get foreigners down here. We were used to right-hand drive engines, firing from the left-hand side, and of course the BR standards were left-hand drive – took quite a bit of getting used to.'

John made one interesting point about preparation and disposal. During his time as a fireman there was in force an agreement with the union that firemen would not drop the fire at the end of the shift as it was felt that there might be some risk to eyesight. He was expected to run the fire down and break it up so that the fire dropper could get on with his work as soon as the engine was on the shed. On a Bristol–Exeter run, for instance, know-ing that the engine was going on to the shed at Exeter, the fireman would start to run down his fire after Whiteball tunnel, about twenty miles from Exeter. He would from his know-ledge of the road, the engine, the load and, of course, the driver, know where he could stop firing and start tidying the footplate. This raised another interesting point: although the

35. 'Give me your tea can.' Pannier tank 6411 is ready to leave Chard Central with a Taunton train.

Hugh Ballantyne

Real Photographs Ltd

36. The thrice weekly 10.55 a.m. pick-up goods from Newton Abbot shunts at Trusham, here sadly neglected – 10 August 1961.

fireman did not have to sign for the road, he was expected to be very familiar with it.

'With a good team when the fireman was having a rest he'd be looking out for signals and he'd tell his mate that so-and-so board was off and his mate would repeat it.

'I went from the shunting link into the Bristol–Plymouth goods link. We had the lot there – Halls, Castles, Britannias and Kings on express parcels. Promotion was predictable, if somewhat slow, and I went into what was known as the valleys link. Here we worked the Dulverton branch, the Teign valley, the Moretonhampstead and the Tiverton branches. As a matter of fact it was on the Tiverton branch that I had to drop my own fire and then only if I was late turn Saturdays – there was a man employed five nights a week as a fire dropper. It was all tank engine work –

the 14s were my favourites – and most of it was auto working (push and pull). The stronger version of the 14xx was the 54xx and the 64s were stronger still, propelling and trailing four coaches – you had the engine in the middle sandwiched between the coaches. On auto working the fireman spent a lot of time on his own as the driver was in the front compartment of the auto coach. The regulator was mechanically connected by rods to the engine and the driver had a brake. Communication was by a bell code and all that the fireman did was blow off the brake and fire the loco. I liked the Dulverton trip. It was twenty-five miles from Exeter, most of it uphill and fairly hard, but for the return I'd build up the fire at Dulverton and there was no need to touch it again until we were almost into Exeter.'

*Hugh Ballantyne*

*G. R. Sviour*

37. On a happier June morning in 1958, with the promise of a hot day to come, pannier tank 3677 is ready to leave Christow with the early morning train to Exeter.

Returning to the more practical and routine part of crew training – and the following account was common to all footplate men – the company allocated preparation time according to the size and type of locomotive that was to be prepared: one hour for a 63xx class, forty-five minutes for a 45xx class and one and a quarter hours for Castles and Kings. Thus, if a crew was allocated to say a King, driver and fireman would book on duty one and a quarter hours before the departure time of the train. The driver would spend some time reading notices relevant to the route over which he was to work whilst the fireman would obtain the tool-box keys for the appropriate engine and obtain measured quantities of cylinder and lubricating oil from the stores. On the footplate, the fireman would unlock the tool box, fill up the driver's oil-can and put it to warm. He would then examine the fire and if necessary he would brighten it up by opening the blower and judiciously using the short poker. Before leaving the footplate to carry out his inspection of other parts of the engine, the fireman would check the water level in the boiler.

In theory, driver and fireman should have arrived at the engine together; in fact what usually happened was that the fireman arrived first and carried out part of the preparation procedures. In some instances, the driver insisted that his mate was there first.

Leaving the footplate, the fireman would go to the front of the engine and open the smokebox door. He would check that the front tubeplate cover was in position and secured, that the blast-pipe jumper ring was loose and free to move and he would sweep away any smokebox char left behind by the cleaners. He would then check the washout plugs and finally close the smokebox door, ensuring that it was a tight fit. Any air leaks around the smokebox door seal would adversely affect the steaming of the engine and would upset the driver!

The fireman would then inspect the sand boxes and sand pipes. The former had to be full of dry sand and the latter in position in front of the coupled wheels. If sand was required it had to be carried from the drying furnace and lifted on to the running plate from rail level – quite a feat as the Kings had 6 ft. 6 in. coupled wheels.

At this point, the driver would require his fireman to be on the footplate and would indeed have him at his beck and call.

Now the fireman would begin to bring his fire round whilst the driver went underneath the engine to begin the routine of oiling the big ends, eccentrics, valve gear, combining lever, guide link, valve spindles and so on. He would need the reverser to be moved to enable him to reach all the moving parts, hence his insistence that the fireman was on the footplate. The driver would then turn his attention to the outside motion, slide bars, crosshead, outside big end – and to the axle boxes. The chances are that the engine was not correctly positioned to enable the driver to reach all the oiling points and it might well have to be moved – another good reason for the fireman being on the footplate.

Whilst the driver was carrying out his oiling and inspection, the fireman would have brought the boiler pressure up from the 50–60 lb. per square inch when he took over to 160–180 lb. per square inch, at which point it would be safe to move the engine should the driver so require. It should perhaps be explained that in the case of a vacuum-braked engine, where the brakes are applied by destroying the vacuum and allowing air into the system, a fairly high boiler pressure is needed for the ejector to be able to create sufficient

38. Two Collett 0–4–2Ts at Tiverton on 30 May 1959.
On the left 1471 enters with the 5.30 p.m.
Dulverton–Exeter, whilst 1440 waits in the bay with the
Tiverton junction train.

*S. C. Nash*

vacuum for the brakes to work. It was, I was told, a very foolish man who would move a big engine with less than say 120 lb. per square inch showing on the pressure gauge, and indeed I felt very foolish having done just that on one – and only one – occasion. 146 tons of locomotive, moving at even less than walking pace, takes a lot of stopping on the tender handbrake. I had been in charge of disposal of the engine, I had run the fire down and left enough steam pressure to hold the brakes off and to move under the coaling hoist. I misjudged the point at which to stop and in stopping destroyed the vacuum and there was not enough boiler pressure to re-create it. Then came the calculated risk – move her a touch and have a man on the tender brake. She moved well enough – just a flick of the regulator and she was off. With three of us on the handbrake the engine travelled some fifteen yards before stopping.

To return to the preparation of a locomotive, the fireman has trimmed the coal in the tender and thrown forward the coal that he needs to build up the fire to its maximum. He has checked his fire irons not only to ensure that he has a full set but also to ensure that they are safely stowed away. Some of the earlier types of Great Western tender had fire-iron racks along one side, and handling the long poker and bent dart, both about twelve feet long, posed problems for the fireman. Indeed, some have been injured whilst taking the long irons out of the rack when the handle, protruding over the tender side or above the cab roof, has struck a bridge abutment. One incident related to me concerned a fireman who unfortunately got the long poker tangled in telegraph wires and both he and the poker left the footplate rather hurriedly. The driver braked hard, stopped the train and dropped off the footplate only to meet his

39. All is neatness and industry in this picture of Christow in 1920.

Ian Allan Ltd

40. Castle 7003, 'Elmley Castle', with a train for Kingswear passes 2—10—0 92207 waiting for the road with a Bristol—Plymouth fitted freight.

mate walking back along the track with the poker over his shoulder. He had, apparently, gone straight off the engine, over the fence and into a field. All that was damaged was his dignity. To prevent this sort of incident happening too often, modifications were made to locomotive designs so that the fire irons were stored in a tunnel alongside the boiler.

Having attended to the safety aspects of the coal and the fire irons, the fireman next tests the injectors and he is joined by the driver, who has completed his oiling by checking the tender axle-boxes and oiling the water pickup apparatus. The driver opens the large ejector and watches the two indicator needles on his brake gauge. One, on the train pipe side, should register 25 inches of mercury, the other on the reservoir side, 22 inches. At those readings he applies the brake, destroys the vacuum and then re-creates it. He next checks the flow of oil through the inspection glasses of the hydrostatic lubricator and once he has satisfied himself that there is a flow of between fourteen and eighteen drops of oil per

minute, the fireman tops up the tender tank with water and the engine is ready to leave the shed.

Senior cleaners were allocated firing turns on shunting duties and were trained by the drivers. These were invariably men of vast experience, nearing the end of their careers, who had been taken off main-line duties for health reasons, usually eyesight problems. When the cleaner was ready to be promoted to the passed cleaner grade, a firing inspector would examine him on rules and, if successful, the cleaner would be designated passed cleaner and then would be available for firing turns.

'No two men', said John Twitchen, 'fire exactly alike. Footplate relationships were very important and if the driver had confidence in his mate there was no great problem, but a driver who interfered was no great help and could make things worse. On my first London trip I was rostered to fill in for a man who was off sick. We had a Castle — and when the driver discovered that I hadn't worked a

W. Philip Conolly

41. The overall roof of Exeter St Thomas station casts a striking pattern on 2–6–0 6301 hauling a mixed freight on 10 June 1956.

London before he went to the shed foreman and said that he wouldn't go with me, but there was nobody else so he hadn't much choice. His regular mate had been with him for six years and could probably anticipate when the driver was going to blow his nose so as far as I was concerned he was very anti. As the trip proceeded and he could see that I knew what I was doing he relaxed, we had a good run and got on quite well. It was only a one-way job. We were off Newton at 4.30 p.m. Saturday, due in Paddington at 9.15 p.m., and we came back on the cushions next day. I suppose I understood how he felt – I had a regular mate for four years.'

He quoted another example of footplate relationships and the only time that he was reported:

'We were coming from Taunton and we stopped for a banker at Wellington to get us over Whiteball. In the tunnel, the driver decided to have a joke and lose the banker so he opened up and knocked the fire about. As a result, we ran out of steam and stopped the 5.30 p.m. London. A few days later he told me that he'd sent in a report blaming his fireman. There wasn't much that I could do about it so I shrugged it off.'

At this point John's regular mate interposed with a tale from his own experience about the tank engines that worked the branches.

'There was a 64 on passenger pilot work at Exeter that was condemned for main-line working. One morning it was standing in a siding whilst its crew had breakfast in the shunters' cabin. A 14xx came off the shed and as a result of poor preparation it had a green

64

fire so the crew swapped engines – took the 64 and left the 14 without anybody's knowledge or consent. They worked to Tiverton and back with the condemned 64 – the axle boxes had been wedged, the tubes and stays were unsafe and it hadn't exceeded 5 mph for some time. Somehow it got back to Exeter, where the crew promptly swapped it for the diagrammed 14xx.

'The passenger pilot driver, blissfully unaware of what had happened, finished his breakfast and went to climb up on to his engine. He couldn't help but notice the smoke coming from the big ends and axle boxes and realised that the loco wasn't safe, even for shunting. He contacted the loco foreman and it's a great pity their conversation wasn't taped for posterity.'

John then gave an example of one of his working days.

'Book on at 6.30 a.m. and take the 7 a.m. Exeter–Heathfield. Here we'd change with a Newton Abbot crew and work to Moretonhampstead, then Moretonhampstead to Paignton, Paignton back to Heathfield, swap with the same Newton Abbot crew and work to Exeter via the Teign valley. We had our trials and tribulations. I remember working the 9.30 p.m. Saturday off Exeter up the Teign valley. This was the last train up the branch and it returned to Exeter via Newton Abbot and the main line. The engine had been out since 2 p.m. and had done two trips to Dulverton when we got it. We had two coaches on and it's a long pull from City Basin to Longdown. By Perridge tunnel we were twenty minutes down and the water was getting low. Of course, the slower we went the more trouble I had with the brakes – they were leaking on and the pump wasn't working

42. Not long after construction Castle 4074, 'Caldicot Castle', enters Paddington with a train from the west of England.

fast enough to keep them off. We had to stop at Longdown for a blow up. Eventually we did stagger to Exeter. All this was due to a dirty fire. Once it happens there's not much hope. It was usually due to poor quality fuel and as a result clinker would form on the bars.

'The BR standards gave me some of my nastiest moments. The only blow back that I experienced was quite minor but it was a BR standard that did it. Of course, it was a tunnel, we were on the drift and forgot the blower. As a result I had my hair and eyebrows singed. We got used to them after a while and if we were coming up to Marley tunnel it was almost routine to lift the fall plate between the cab and the tender. If you didn't do this, you'd almost choke to death in the cab.

'Of course, the job had its lighter side. I remember being rostered to a Plymouth freight one Good Friday. It was a one way only job – back on the cushions – and it was a slow one. We were put inside at South Brent

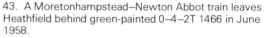

43. A Moretonhampstead–Newton Abbot train leaves Heathfield behind green-painted 0–4–2T 1466 in June 1958.

and I decided to gather some primroses. I dropped off the engine, lost my footing and fell down the bank and lost interest in primroses. Eventually we got to Plymouth and the signalman told us that there was nothing back from Laira to North Road. We knew if we didn't get back to North Road fairly quickly we'd miss our connection for Exeter and it was standing in North Road. But then we spotted an empty stock train on its way to North Road. It had a West Country on it but the driver wasn't for stopping. He shouted to us that he'd slow down and we could scramble on. This was all right except that I overlooked the cant on the curve and as I grabbed a door on one of the coaches and pulled myself up it swung outwards, and I was hanging on for dear life. Fortunately my mate pulled me into the coach, but I began to have the feeling it wasn't my day.'

# 8
# The Guards

The glamour belongs – rightly, I suppose – to the footplate men, particularly to the drivers. Even the driver of a pick-up goods had some prestige – he was, after all, an engine driver. But what of the guards? The passenger guard inevitably had his moment of glory as departure time approached. The watch, the whistle, the green flag, the response from the engine, and then as the train began to move he would with consummate nonchalance do something that everyone else was specifically forbidden to do: he would board a moving train. He would stand casually, framed in the doorway of *his* compartment as the train gathered speed, stepping back and closing his door – and even his door was special as it was the only one on the train that opened inwards – as the train cleared the end of the platform. What then? Well, he retired to his private world, equipped with a swivelling armchair, a desk, his personal vacuum gauge and brake handle and a massive handbrake wheel with its formidable ratchet. If, on passing through the train, one stole a quick glance into this private world, its remote occupant might deign to acknowledge one's presence with a nod. More than likely he would be consulting his watch and making an entry in his journal. The journey over, he could be seen walking unhurriedly and with dignity down the platform. On his shoulder was the large leather bag that was one of the badges of his office and, protruding from it, three carefully furled flags. Was the yellow one ever used? In one hand the guard carried the ultimate in badges of office – his hand lamp. And so he walked down the ramp and disappeared towards his booking-off point.

But how different, how much less esoteric was the lot of the goods guard. Not for him the swivel armchair in a comfortably heated compartment. He had to be content with a draughty van heated by a coal-fired stove. He was marooned at the end of a loose-coupled train, constantly jostled and shaken about, trying to fill in his journal or prepare his food by the light of his hand lamp, ever hopeful that the train might be turned inside, thus giving him some respite.

Think of the goods guard on a wet, cold and windy night, climbing from his van, stumbling along the ballast and pinning down the brakes of the wagons in the train for which he is responsible. Think of him supervising shunting operations at 4 a.m. on a winter's morning.

Cecil Sussex joined the GWR as a porter in October 1918, became a goods guard in 1942 and a passenger guard in 1960, retiring in 1966.

'When I look back over the years,' he told me, 'I see what a great change has taken place in discipline of the staff. One case stands out in my memory. In 1920 I was a porter at Ilminster station on the Chard branch. While I was pasting bills on the boards on the platform a lady asked me for a train service from Ilminster to Weston-super-Mare for tomorrow and back the day after. I looked at the timetable and put the services on a piece of paper and handed it to her. She said thank you and went on her way. Some week or ten days after, the Chief Divisional Inspector from Exeter arrived and called all the staff into the office one at a time. It came to my turn and I was asked did I remember if I had given a lady information regarding a train service to Weston. I answered that I did. What day was it – can you remember? No, sir, I cannot. Did you know that the day after tomorrow was a Sunday when there is no service on the Chard branch? No, sir, I never gave it a thought. The lady took the train from Weston-super-Mare to Taunton, found no trains to Ilminster so took a taxi and sent the bill to the Superintendent at Exeter! I had to make out a report and send it to Exeter and after a few more days a pass arrived and I had to go to see the Superintendent, who tore me off a strip and finally said that he was going to give me one day's suspension and that would be today.

'My reply was: I beg your pardon, sir, but I have worked today and expect to be paid for it, I will have tomorrow off. His reply was get out of his office. So my mistake in giving wrong information cost me one day's pay. I wonder what action would be taken today by BR and by the trade union?' Cecil left the question unanswered.

Following his time as a porter, Cecil was transferred to Hackney Yard at Newton Abbot as a shunter. At the time there were twenty-eight shunters at Hackney and a spirit of competition existed amongst the inspectors as to which shunting gang could marshal and dispatch a train the quickest.

In 1925 a shunter at Torre was dismissed for stealing cigarettes and Cecil went to Torre, staying there until 1939 when he returned to Hackney. In 1942, in response to an application made sometime before, he was made a goods guard.

As with many aspects of railway work at ground level, the training of guards was essentially practical and it seems, to the layman at least, quite minimal. In Cecil's case, and there is no reason to think that his training was different from that of any other goods guard, he was allowed three days to learn each of the following roads: Newton Abbot—Plymouth, Newton Abbot—Bristol and the South Devon branch lines to Kingswear, Ashburton, Moretonhampstead, Kingsbridge and the Teign Valley. In each case he spent the three days with an experienced guard, working the same train on each occasion. The emphasis was on learning the gradients, learning the signals, knowing where to apply the handbrake and where to get down from the van and pin down the brakes on individual wagons.

Following this period of instruction, the new aspirant to the clan was examined by the Divisional Inspector. This was an oral examination based on rules and on situations that the DI would invent. Assuming that all went well, the newly qualified guard would be interviewed by the line superintendent and he would then be out on the road. Unlike the drivers, who were tested on rules once and once only, guards were tested every two

44. 2–6–0 7337 accelerates a mixed down freight past Victory sidings between Norton Fitzwarren and Wellington.

years – this underlines the point that it is the guard who is in charge of the train, not the driver.

An illustration of this happened when Cecil was guard on a cattle train from Hackney Yard to Ashburton. Operating expediency decreed that the cattle trucks should be attached to the Ivybridge goods train but the load proved to be too much for the 44xx tank engine and it failed at Dainton bank. The Ivybridge goods guard was technically in charge of the train and he immediately went back to protect the rear of the train by placing detonators on the track. Meanwhile, Cecil went to the engine to check with the driver and was told that the fireman had been sent to Dainton Box for a wrong line order. This would allow a pilot engine to be coupled to the disabled 44xx but, as Cecil pointed out, all

available spare engines were at Totnes behind the train. Therefore a wrong line order was unnecessary – all that was required was a phone call from Dainton to Totnes. The fireman now had to return to the signal-box, go through the procedure of cancelling the wrong line order and then phone for a banker to push the train over Dainton Summit. What should have been a 15-minute delay was in fact a 45-minute delay and it occurred because the driver did not consult his guard before taking action.

Cecil also relates, in his delightful South Devon accent that the written word cannot hope to evoke, an incident which, while amusing, could have had serious consequence.

'I was rostered to a ballast train for Westbury, leaving Hackney at 11.55 p.m. Sunday. They told me that there was no return working

D. E. Esau

45. A vandalised Hall 6916, almost at the end of its career, hauls a curiously mixed freight near Ruabon in 1965.

and that I could come back on the 10.10 p.m. Banbury goods, off Westbury about 4 a.m. Well, we got there all right and the three of us – driver, fireman and myself – hung about waiting for the Banbury. We got into the brake van and away we went. We all settled down to have a sleep and after about half an hour the fireman got up and went out on the veranda at the end of the van. He came back in and said, "Don't know whether it makes any difference, but we ain't got a damned engine." Now I knew this lad to be a regular leg-puller and didn't take much notice. But he didn't sit down – he hung on to the hand rail. I got up and looked out and sure enough we were bowling along at about 35 mph and not an engine in sight. We all went for the handbrake and eventually brought the train to a stop. The guard gets down and goes along the train counting the trucks. Back he comes. "We got eighty-one," he says. "We

left with eighty-two so he's gone off with one."

'"You'll have to back to Cary and arrange for assistance from the rear," I told him. But the guard said that he wouldn't walk all the way – all the boxes were switched out as it was Sunday. He walked back to the nearest box, broke a window and got on the phone. They didn't like that at all – he got into trouble for breaking into that box. While he's doing this, the driver and the fireman and me picked wild strawberries. Eventually an engine came out from Cary and pushed us to Athelney. The train engine was there waiting for us. He'd no option but to keep going when he discovered that he'd lost his train. It's a fairly easy road and the 28xx loco was making light work of it so the driver wouldn't necessarily notice that he'd lost his train. Of course, he'd no idea where it had come off or how far it was behind him and he was on the approach to Sommerton tunnel so he had to keep going. The signalman at Athelney had set the road to turn us down the branch to Ling Halt. We eventually got back to Newton at about four in the afternoon. It was a broken coupling that caused it. I expect that there was an inquiry but I didn't hear anything about it.'

Such were the guard's responsibilities that if he felt that the load of the train was too much for the engine provided, he could – and did – refuse to go. In calculating the load of a train, rule of thumb guidelines were handed on from one generation of guards to the next: three trucks of goods = two of coal; two emptics = one of coal; and a 28xx must not be allowed to take more than thirty-seven trucks of mineral over Dainton.

The routine work of the goods guard was instanced by one particular turn: book on at 3.40 a.m. to work the 4.15 a.m. pick-up goods train to Exeter. This consisted of five station trucks plus any others for Exeter and beyond. The guard would check each truck – destination labels, contents, couplings and brakes – and then advise the driver of the number of trucks and the total weight of the train. The train, always accompanied by a shunter, would leave via the main line for Exeter, calling at Teignmouth, Dawlish, Dawlish Warren, Starcross and Exminster. At each station the station truck would be shunted and at Dawlish Warren the train would be turned inside – diverted on to the slow line – to Exminster where a stop was made for breakfast, usually a fry-up on the guard's van stove. At each stopping-point the guard would make sure that the freight that was

unloaded was at its correct destination and so, when the train arrived in Exeter, all that remained was freight for Exeter. The return working was the 9 a.m. Exeter–Hackney Yard and it was exactly the reverse of the up working. The guard would be rostered to this particular turn for a week.

Occasionally, very occasionally, something would happen to break the monotony. Let Cecil Sussex relate this in his own words:

'On an early date in June 1947, having changed turns with another guard, I was booked to work the 12.30 p.m. from Hackney Yard to Brixham. Leaving Hackney right time we arrived at the stop board situated about half a mile the Newton Abbot side of Torre station at 1.02 p.m. I walked to the front of the train and applied hand brakes until I got a signal from the driver that he now had enough brake power to descend the incline in safety. I then returned to the rear and was about to join my van when it was actually knocked from my grasp by the engine of a down express. [What a masterly piece of understatement!] My van was thrown on its side on the opposite line, completely blocking the up main. When the impact took place I jumped across a four-foot watercourse and landed several feet up the bank out of harm's way. The fireman of the down express grabbed flags and detonators and was on his way to protect the opposite road; his driver, B. C. Pope, shouted to him, "Gordon, look in the van before you go." His reply was: "It's OK Bert, the guard is on the bank." He [the driver] at once fainted with relief, thankful that he had not killed the guard. He was taken to Torbay hospital and not released until 8 p.m. Only two passengers on the train were slightly injured, neither requiring treatment. The passenger train was pulled back to Newton Abbot and passengers conveyed to their destinations by an arranged bus service.'

'How did this happen?'

'A passenger train had arrived at Torre. It was too long for the signalman to see the tail lamp but he could and did look back to a mirror fixed on a pole for that purpose, saw the reflection of the tail lamp and immediately cleared the block section and gave line clear to the home signal for the goods train. Several minutes later the passenger train in the station drew ahead to unload the rear part of the train which had not been on the platform. As it stopped, the signalman, now actually seeing the tail lamp, cleared the section again and accepted the down express. So now he had three trains under his care on one line. At the time there were two signalmen in the box at Torre, one was in charge and one was learning the box and of course it could be, if there was a certain amount of talking going on, the reason why the signalman in charge made that awful mistake.'

At the time that Cecil Sussex was looking for promotion from goods guard to passenger guard, the goods guards were permitted to apply only for one vacancy in four when passenger guards retired or left the company. Thus promotion was slow and in some cases non-existent. Vacancies were advertised throughout the division and the man who was prepared to move home and family was the man most likely to be promoted.

Vacancies were well contested as the job had many advantages over its less glamorous goods counterpart. There was wider scope for travel, working conditions were much more congenial and there was of course a mileage bonus.

Compare the working of a Newton Abbot–Paddington express passenger train with the 4.15 a.m. pick-up goods. The guard booked on duty, walked through the train noting the types of coaches, lot numbers and weights, and he passed this information on to the driver. When the train was on the move the guard checked the van contents – parcels, luggage, mail and so on and then walked through the train counting the passengers. This count had to be accurate, it had to be entered in the guard's journal and was carried out at Exeter, Taunton and Westbury. (It could and did cause some embarrassment, particularly on night trains!) Passing times were noted at Exeter, Whiteball, Taunton, Castle Cary, Westbury, Didcot and Reading and meticulously entered in the journal. If time was lost it had to be noted and the reason given. Signals? Permanent way restriction? Defective locomotive? Or was it due to the driver? If, in the guard's opinion, time lost was due to poor driving, the lost time was booked against the driver and entered on his record.

The value of the guard's journal – or log – was beyond question. Or was it?

'I was rostered', said Cecil, 'to an empty stock working out of Paignton to Bristol. I dumped my kit in the van and then walked through, checking weights and numbers. Having done this, I then went to the front brake compartment to check the handbrake but as soon as I slid open the door Mr Ben, the bloody cat from Paignton station, jumped out – he'd been shut in overnight. It put me off and I shut the door without checking the brake. The engine came on to the train, the shunter coupled him and then rode with me to Paignton station. As we were going through Newton I thought that one of the platform staff looked a bit peculiar at the train and then we were brought to a stop at Bishopsteignton. I've never seen anything like it. All the lubrication had melted and we'd been throwing

M. J. Fox

sparks all the way. Of course I realised what had happened – I'd forgotten the handbrake. Well, the bearing seemed to be OK so we went on to Exeter and the carriage and wagon examiner had a look at it and, luckily, all was well. I logged the incident but I forgot to give it in and it was never mentioned again.'

46. Imagine the guard's feelings as, banked by a Hymek diesel, his freight climbs Wellington bank at Beam Bridge hauled by Hall 4932, 'Hatherton Hall'.

# 9
# The Signalmen

Teigngrace, Trusham, Longdown and Ide (pronounced 'Eed') may not be as euphonious as Sir John Betjeman's Rime Intrinsica, Fontwell Magna, Sturminster Newton and Melbury Bubb, but the railway line that connected them would, in its heyday, have moved the Poet Laureate to dash off a half-dozen verses in praise of what was a typical GWR branch line.

The Teign Valley line, for so it was called, connected Exeter St Davids with Heathfield Junction, whence there was a line to Newton Abbot, and the trains that served the branch wound their way alongside the river Teign and through attractive countryside. Even a very wet February day did not altogether obscure the beauties of the route and, where traces of the track bed are visible, it is not too difficult to imagine a 14xx, complete with auto coach – yes, only one – waiting for the signal at Heathfield or working hard as it climbed towards Perridge tunnel.

Reference to the 1938 summer timetable reveals that there were nine trains per weekday in each direction with an extra one on Saturday evenings through to Newton Abbot.

The Exeter men, when asked what they remembered about the Teign Valley line, agreed that it was one of the most picturesque branches on which they had worked. Comments were made such as 'You could always get your pea sticks out there' and 'Do you remember the daffodil specials?' It seems that before the Second World War excursions were run on Sundays from Exeter to Christow at a charge of 6d (2½p) per person. At Christow the train was shunted into the loop where it remained until the advertised return time. Families would take advantage of the service to have a picnic in the country and to pick daffodils that grew in abundance in the fields and woods along the sides of the line. Mushrooms were another feature of the line. These were easily seen from the elevated position of the footplate by an alert crew. An unscheduled stop would be made, the fireman would drop quickly from the footplate nip over the fence, fill his greasetop cap with mushrooms and then jump equally quickly back on the engine.

Apart from serving the communities scattered along the banks of the Teign, the branch was a useful avoiding route when there were problems on the main line between Exeter City Basin and Newton Abbot. Closure of the branch in 1959 implied that main-line problems no longer exist.

Longdown station is – or was – situated on

a curve and between two tunnels. The station buildings remain, as do the tunnels, the latter in a remarkably good state of repair. Little remains of the track bed although the ballast is visible in one or two places. Rising steeply from behind the station buildings is a well wooded embankment that leads towards the entrance of Perridge tunnel, while immediately in front of the station and opposite the platform is another wooded embankment that drops away into fields and leads eventually to the entrance of Culver tunnel. Thus Longdown station is bounded by trees and tunnels, an eerie spot that might well have formed the setting for Arnold Ridley's *The Ghost Train*.

Under the conditions governing its pur-chase, the land on which the line was built had on closure to be offered to its original owner or descendants thereof. It so happened that a direct descendant of the original owner of the Longdown section lived, and happily still lives, within sight of the station and he resumed ownership. The station buildings fell into disrepair: Perridge tunnel is used for mushroom cultivation on a commercial scale and the site would no doubt have been cleared had it not been for the efforts of a group of preservationists from Exeter which has, with the blessing and co-operation of the owner, undertaken a long-term and expensive restoration scheme. A fully restored GWR branch line station minus track and, *ipso facto*, trains

W. Philip Conolly

47. GWR lower quadrant signals at the north end of Shrewsbury station.

does seem rather odd; two of the stations farther down the branch towards Heathfield have been converted into houses – that at Christow is outstanding, the owner having gone to no small amount of trouble to preserve the station atmosphere – and there can be no question of the line ever being opened again. But one can only marvel at the dedication of the Longdown enthusiasts.

Although this book is primarily about footplate and operating experiences it would, I feel, have been churlish and ungrateful to ignore signalmen. After all, without the signalmen the trains don't move. By good fortune I was able to talk to three generations of signalmen who had worked in Longdown Box and whose service spanned the years from 1922 to the closure of the branch in 1959. Not for them the hustle and bustle of life in, say, Newton Abbot East, but a leisurely sort of existence that was remarkably unchanged over thirty-seven years. Romantically, they give us glimpses of a way of life that has disappeared – a settled and stable community, a predictable pattern of events. Economically it had, of course, to come to an end.

Tom Way joined the GWR as a messenger boy at Exeter in 1914, retiring from railway service in 1965, at which time he was signalman at Paignton North.

In 1922 Longdown was a class six box – at the time that was the lowest classification and classification was based upon the number of

48. Christow station in May 1978 – a view from the same bridge as photo 39 on page 62.

Author

G. R. Siviour

lever movements, bell signals, book entries and so on that a signalman made in one standard shift of eight hours. Then, as now, if a man felt that his box was underrated he could ask for it to be reassessed, but this always carried the risk that the inspector carrying out the check might decide that the box should be down-graded. There was no chance of down-grading at Longdown, where the signalman was booking clerk and porter in addition to operating the box.

Earlier in this chapter the 1938 timetable was quoted – it hardly changed from before the First World War – but the early 1920s did see some freight traffic up and down the branch from Christow and Trusham. It seems, however, that the most important freight was the wagon that brought in coal for Culver House and for which a siding was put in. Such was the dominance of the squirearchy in rural communities.

Passenger traffic consisted of one or two commuters to Exeter and of schoolchildren, and in the time between trains Tom grew plants in the station garden and in season had flowers for sale. He kept them fresh by displaying them in the station firebuckets.

Winter evenings revived memories of the ghost of Perridge tunnel. Someone had committed suicide in the tunnel and was decapitated in the process. A headless ghost was reputed to haunt the station end of the tunnel and, although no one claims actually to have seen it, Tom Way admitted having been sufficiently alarmed by the very thought to lock himself in the station office.

49. Longdown station in 1958.

H. G. Forsythe

50. Reading West signal box in 1961.

The 1939–45 war gave the branch a new lease of life and its importance as an avoiding route was recognised.

Mervyn Jeans worked at Longdown from 1940 to 1946 and, although the box was upgraded slightly and was open twenty-four hours a day, the routine had varied little from Tom Way's time.

Early in 1941 a passing loop was put in at Longdown, the work being carried out by outside contractors. It seems that the men employed were direct descendants of the railway navvies and created quite a stir in the neighbouring villages. The passing loop was considered necessary because of the increasing importance of the branch as an avoiding

line. Rumour had it that it was the intention of the German Navy to send a submarine to torpedo the sea wall at Dawlish, a feat that would no doubt have earned the intrepid U-boat commander the Iron Cross. But scoff as we may from this distance, the rumour was treated seriously enough for the passing loop to be installed and for Mervyn Jeans to spend his night shifts sleeping on the office floor, deriving some comfort from the fact that he was being paid for sleeping.

The entry of the USA into the war following Pearl Harbour meant that no longer were Merv Jeans's nights guaranteed to be undisturbed. An American military hospital was built at Heathfield and ambulance trains ran

51. A general view of the same signal box at an earlier, unknown date. Note the gas lights.

*British Rail*

as required, always at night, and always as silently as possible and in total darkness. Blackout conditions did not mean much at Longdown and that is perhaps why the impressive feature about the ambulance trains was their total darkness.

The war ended, nationalisation came, and although the Teign Valley line passed from GWR ownership little had changed in the years from 1922.

After having been a booking boy at Newton Abbot West, Dave Bright received his preferment and was appointed acting porter-signalman at Longdown in 1956. His duties were fairly well defined, particularly when he was on early turn. This meant leav-

ing home in Newton Abbot at 5.45 a.m. in order to book on and open that station at 6.20 a.m. He then had to light the Tilly lamps so that he could see to make tea for the crew of the first train from Exeter. This was a most important duty as good working relations with the branch-line train crews were essential if the signalman wanted to get away on time on Saturday evenings. Following this, the platforms, waiting rooms and office had to be swept and once a month came the additional duty of pumping water from a well on the station into a tank to supply the lavatories. (Drinking water was brought by train in cans from Trusham.) Then it was time for a leisurely breakfast and the morning

79

might be interspersed with the arrival of a passenger, although these rarities were regarded not as a welcome break in a dull routine but as something of an intrusion. As Dave pointed out, two or three passengers per month was about par for the course and two in one week he still remembers!

The Suez crisis with attendant rationing of petrol brought a variation and break in routine. Always a keen motorcyclist, Dave arranged with his opposite number to work alternate shifts in an attempt to save petrol and to preserve his coupons. Thus he would work a late turn, sleep in the station office, work an early turn and then go home. He speaks with not a little nostalgia of midsummer evenings when he would, between trains, walk in the woods and explore the surrounding countryside. He relates how a guard persuaded him to collect bundles of pea sticks, a job that Dave was pleased to do until he discovered that the guard was selling them on Exeter market. Dark, misty and frosty winter evenings were another matter however. From time to time, local people would drop in for a chat and invariably conversation would centre around doings in the village, the big house and the ghost. One night, having locked up and made up his bed, Dave was about to settle down when he heard a noise on the platform. Screwing his courage to its sticking point, he cautiously opened the door and shone the beam of his lamp outside. It illuminated the somewhat dirty, and weatherbeaten face of the local pig man, standing motionless, patch over one eye – he'd decided to pay a social call.

On another occasion, one of Dave's motorcycling friends had ridden out from Newton Abbot with the ingredients for a fry-up. Deciding that the meal would be incomplete without potatoes, a quick foray was made into an adjacent field and the meal was duly cooked and eaten. Towards midnight, the friend returned to Newton Abbot and Dave prepared for the night. Flop, flop, flop along the platform; pangs of conscience; had someone seen them lifting potatoes? Could it be the pig man again? There it was – flop, flop, flop. Slow, deliberate footsteps. It couldn't be the ghost – could it? Unable to stand the suspense Dave flung open the door, shone his handlamp along the platform and 'there was the biggest bloody frog you ever saw, hopping along the platform'.

Late turn on Saturdays was never popular. The last train was off Longdown at 9.26 p.m. and then ten minutes had to elapse before the line could be cleared to Christow. If Dave was on his motorcycle this didn't present much difficulty, but if he was short of petrol or the weather was particularly bad he had problems getting home.

There was, he told me, little to choose between the early turn – from 6.20 to 13.58 – and the late turn – from 13.58 to 21.26. Both were equally dead. There were irksome routines to be followed such as filling in the

52 (*right*). Severn Tunnel East signal box. The apprehensive expression on the signalman's face is more than justified, since the photograph was taken using flash powder; too much was used and the windows of the box were almost blown out!

Noël Ingram

81

passenger returns, almost invariably nil, securing this vital information in a locked leather pouch and handing it to the guard of the first train of the day and receiving with due solemnity an empty leather pouch for the coming day's returns. Then there was the business of the hurricane lamps in the winter. These had to be lit and placed at prescribed points along the platform before the arrival of each train in each direction during the hours of darkness and removed and extinguished after the trains had departed.

According to Dave Bright Longdown was no place for a young man, but as he showed me around and as we walked the track together it was clear that the coming generation of signalmen will not be able to share the experience of working on a rural branch line. They will miss something.

53. At the north end of Shrewsbury station on 28 August 1952. Hall 4976, 'Warfield Hall', is on the Hastings–Birkenhead train, Stanier 8F 48706 is on a freight for Crewe, and Saint 2933, 'Bibury Court', is on the 4.50 p.m. to Gobowen.

# 10
# Heirs of the Great Western

Brian Morrison

Since the inception of the Torbay Steam Railway in 1973 I have spent many happy hours working as a volunteer in the locomotive department at Queen's Park Station, Paignton. Through the good offices of Barry Cogar, the General Manager, and with the wholehearted co-operation of Nat Clifford, the Company's Mechanical Engineer, I was able to conduct two interviews, one on the footplate of 'Lydham Manor' as she worked a seven-coach train to Kingswear and back, the other in the cab of 1638 as she worked five coaches from Buckfastleigh to Totnes and back.

The two lines are almost identical in length but they vary dramatically in scenery and in the nature of the road. I joined Stan Turner and his fireman Peter 'Jesse' Janes on the footplate of 'Lydham Manor' about twenty minutes before the train was due to leave and we talked about their respective backgrounds. Stan Turner joined the LNER as a cleaner in 1947, was driving by 1957, and then in 1969 became redundant. He spent four years as a window cleaner and joined the TSR in 1973. 'Jesse' Janes joined the company during the same year as a fitter and he was warned at the time that he might be called upon to do other jobs – a small com-

pany has to diversify its resources – and within a few days he was firing. Since then he has qualified as a fireman and is now a passed fireman and acts as a rest-day relief driver. Volunteer footplate work is not allowed on the TSR because of the proximity of the line to BR lines. Thus the footplate crews have to have medicals, undergo a two-hour theory examination and have a practical test on the line. These are all conducted by BR staff and are as stringent as those for BR personnel. The situation on the Dart Valley line is slightly different as volunteer firemen are not only allowed but encouraged. Even so, they are passed by BR inspectors before being allowed to work an engine.

A rapidly filling tender tank abruptly ended our conversation. Stan turned off the water supply, I climbed on to the tender and removed the hose and we moved on to the train. A groundframe, the operation of which is released by a plunger in Paignton South Box, controls the points covering the exit from Queen's Park station. Jesse dropped from the engine, had a word with Dave Bright, the signalman, and then set the road for Stan. As 'Lydham Manor' moved slowly past the groundframe, Jesse shouted to Stan to imagine that he was coming out of

Copenhagen tunnel. We were away on time and ran easily to Goodrington. During the time that we were stopped, Jesse put several rounds on the fire. We left Goodrington with the pressure gauge showing 230 lb., full regulator and 45 per cent cut-off. Immediately ahead is a stiff climb to Waterside and Stan brought the cut-off back to 30 per cent. As we began to climb, Jesse fired steadily. He was careful to close the doors between each shovelful and equally careful to sweep up afterwards. Into Waterside cutting with the blower and the injector both on. Jesse explained that the fireman's prime job is to watch the water level and keep the fire-box crown covered. Closing the fire-box doors between each shovelful of coal limits the amount of cold air entering the fire-box which would adversely affect the boiler pressure.

As we passed the site of the turntable at Churston I noticed that the boiler pressure

54. GWR steam preserved. Manor 7827, 'Lydham Manor', passes Paignton South with a Torbay Steam Railway train for Kingswear.

was dropping slightly. Jesse explained that this was quite deliberate as he didn't want to risk blowing the canopy off Churston station!

During the stop at Churston, Jesse was busy with the slacker pipe, hosing down the footplate. 'With Greenway tunnel ahead,' said Jesse, 'it acts as a vacuum cleaner and the cab is full of dust in no time if you don't hose down.'

We left Churston with the regulator on the first valve and the cut-off at 45 per cent. As we drifted down towards Greenway I commented on the fact that Jesse hadn't touched the shovel since before Churston.

'Well,' he explained, 'there's not much steam required for the run into Kingswear. If I fired now I'd cause smoke in the station

84

G. F. Bannister

when we arrive and at £40 per ton it's part of my job to conserve as much fuel as I can.'

We ran into Greenway tunnel with the blower just cracked and the fire-box doors open. The light from the fire reflected from the cab fittings and threw well defined shadows on the smoke-grimed roof. The noise level precluded conversation and there was something eerie and mysterious about the situation but we were soon out into daylight and dropping down to river level.

Jesse talked about the practical side of his training and was quick to praise the efforts of Stan Turner in this respect. They had done about 8,000 miles a season for three seasons as a team. During that time, they had discussed the rules, Jesse had learnt the anatomy of the steam locomotive and Stan had thought up situations likely to arise for Jesse to solve – a private mutual improvement class.

'On a private railway,' said Jesse, 'where you've saved an engine from scrap, I'm always thinking about the crown of the fire-box. When you consider the cost of lifting this boiler, fitting a new fire-box, taking it out of service, well, that's my job – stopping copper from burning.'

At which point we ran into Kingswear station and had a coffee break. Whilst we were sitting on a seat on the platform a holidaymaker went on to the cab and posed for a photograph. 'Would they', asked Stan, 'get into somebody's car and pose for a photo?'

We ran round the train, coupled up and set off for Paignton tender first. Now the last firing had been at Churston, since when the fire had not been touched, and we still had 210 lb. pressure on leaving Kingswear. The track is level to Britannia Halt and then climbs towards Greenway at 1 in 80. We ran along by the river with the regulator on the

first valve and the cut-off at 20 per cent. This gave us a run at the bank and, as soon as we hit the bottom, the cut-off was adjusted to 30 per cent and the regulator was wide open.

As Jesse was firing steadily, I talked to Stan about his view of the job and the problems associated with it.

'We have to be far more involved on this job than with BR. Here we are concerned with every aspect. The public can be a nuisance at times – I've had to stop to chase them off the track. Even came across one family actually sitting on the track admiring the view. They do things on this railway that they wouldn't dream of doing on BR – take that instance of the photograph in Kingswear. We have to be seen to be policing the line. If we had an accident there'd be a DoE inspector down here like a shot. If we'd been negligent he'd close the line and our livelihoods are at stake. You have to be concerned with every aspect on the TSR – it's not simply a question of driving and firing. We've been fortunate as far as failures on the line are concerned. A spring hanger broke on 4588 on one occasion and we had to lay on a bus service to get the passengers away. We packed the affected spring and brought the train back at reduced speed.'

We were now approaching Churston and as Stan shut off and applied the brake he commented about the increase in popularity of Churston station.

After wishing one of the permanent way gang a happy birthday we were away from Churston on the last lap of the journey. Jesse was tidying up and said that there would be no further firing to be done until leaving Paignton on the return trip – 'Think about fifteen minutes ahead' was his advice.

We drifted down the bank towards Goodrington. Jesse related how he had fired the 'Manor' up the bank on a BR special with twelve coaches on and with Nat Clifford opening and closing the fire-box door for him. He also told me of the occasion when three gauge glasses broke on 4588 in one shift.

'That wouldn't have been so bad,' he said, 'but one of 'em blew when I had my sandwich box open and flooded it.'

'Look at 'em,' he said, with a quick change of emphasis, 'standing by their caravans. I reckon that's all some of 'em do for a fortnight – stand by their caravans and wave to us.'

At that point and with exquisite timing a gust of wind hit the cab at right angles and took Jesse's cap down the embankment. Although this caused some amusement, what was remarkable, according to Stan, was the fact that Jesse was lost for words.

And so into Goodrington. I left the engine and went back into the train to join two of my children with Stan Turner's summary of the job sending me on my way. 'The hardest part of this job is waving.'

The contrast between the two lines is quite remarkable and Nat Clifford's insistence that I should do both sides was quite justified. The TSR follows the coast of Torbay as far as Broadsands. The views are open and quite incomparable and then, following a rural stretch through Churston, the line follows the River Dart again with magnificent views into Kingswear.

The Dart Valley Railway line is totally different in character. It is not scenic in the sense that the TSR is scenic and it meanders alongside the Dart, two stretches of about half a mile each being the straightest sections. Nevertheless, the line has a charm of its own and in one or two places where it runs between a high hedge on one side, luxuriant and

many-shaded after the summer rain, and the peaty brown river on the other side, it conveys a sense of isolation and tranquillity.

I joined Dave Knowling and his fireman, volunteer Chris Woodland, in the cab of 1638 for the 3 p.m. departure from Buckfastleigh on the last Sunday of the 1977 summer time-table. I was accompanied on the trip by Barry Cogar and, although there were four of us on the footplate, the cab was surprisingly roomy. I wedged myself between the lever rack and the cab side and had an excellent view of the road ahead over Dave Knowling's shoulder. Dave has worked for the DVR for over nine years and has been driving for seven. Before joining the company he was with BR as a fireman at Laira and at Old Oak Common.

We left Buckfastleigh on time and ran very well to Nursery Pool Bridge where there was a 5 mph permanent way slack. This was scrupulously observed and 1638 accelerated away very smartly in response to full forward gear and wide open regulator. Chris was having some slight trouble with the fire as the coal was substandard. Although the engine was steaming well it was not up to its usual standard and was using twice the normal quantity of coal. In fact, on the return journey he lost the back corners of the fire. This didn't cause much consternation as there was only one more trip and there was plenty of steam in hand.

Having climbed away from Nursery Pool, Dave shut off and allowed the engine to drift past Shinners Bridge and round the curves into Staverton. We compared the two lines, as far as it is possible to compare them, and Dave made the point that firemen are more often in trouble on the DVR than on the TSR because it is a very deceiving line. 'On the other side,' said Dave, 'you know what to expect, but the gradient on this one varies so much that you can soon be in trouble.'

A large crowd awaited us at Staverton station and, whilst we were waiting for the train to fill, Chris was busy cleaning the fire.

We got away from Staverton and ran briskly towards Totnes. It was obvious that driver and fireman were somewhat concerned about the coal and Dave was careful to conserve his steam. In fact the only time that he used the second valve of the regulator was moving away from the Nursery Pool restriction.

There is some interchange of crews between the TSR and the DVR in so far as Dave goes over to Queen's Park for rest day and holiday relief. He had, he told me, worked for three weeks on the other side this summer.

There are two full-time footplate men at Buckfastleigh and they work turn and turn about as driver and fireman. To enable them to have a rest day, volunteer firemen are used at weekends.

I asked about the attitude of the public towards the line and cited the example that Stan Turner quoted – stopping the train and ushering people off the track. Barry Cogar said that he felt that the DVR is relatively free from such problems because it is out of the way. Having said that, and almost on cue, we rounded a slight curve and there, walking down the track with their backs to us, were two boys. Dave whistled and Barry leaned out of the cab, leaving the unfortunate boys in no doubt that they were trespassing.

We ran easily into what will be Totnes (Riverside), where a brief stop is made at the site of the proposed platform. On the left-hand side of the DVR track is the BR main line and there is a connecting spur. This is, of course, a tremendous advantage and allows movement of stock between the two lines.

The engine ran round the train and before we left for the return journey Chris very

Brian Morrison

55. 7827 running into Paignton Queen's Park station on 6 August 1975. Driver Stan Turner is in charge, assisted by fireman Jesse James.

*J. Everitt*

carefully hosed the coal. Steam pressure was being maintained at about 160 lb. and judicious use of the regulator and reverser kept it there despite problems with the coal.

I asked Dave about incidents and he told me of the time when the train was held up to allow some pigs to finish their meal. A farmer with land on either side of the track was moving a herd of pigs from one field to another and in order to expedite matters, or so he thought, he spread concentrates over the crossing. The pigs refused to move until they'd eaten up!

On another occasion the train was held up because a passenger had lost his false teeth. He had been looking out of the window and his teeth had fallen out. Happily they were recovered.

'It's easily done,' said Dave. 'I suffer from hay fever, and on a firing turn last summer I sneezed and lost my teeth in the coal. Had to wash 'em off with the slacker pipe.'

56 (*top*). 0—6—0 pannier tank 1638 near Staverton on the Dart Valley Railway.

57 (*left*). 1638, in ex-works condition, on shed at Buckfastleigh on the Dart Valley Railway. Note the spare boiler in the background and the boiler and front end of Standard 2—6—4T 80064.

# I I

# Not So Much a Railway –
# More a Way of Life

Brian Morrison

The 1955 Modernisation Plan, branch line closures, inept management, the Beeching Report and the unseemly haste to phase out steam traction meant, inevitably, redundancies. As a typical example, Exeter and Exmouth Junction depots were amalgamated and then policy changes were made that affected the Southern Region: freight workings were phased out, the Salisbury line was single-tracked and Okehampton was closed. Prior to this there were 80 sets of men at Exeter and 250 sets at Exmouth. The option of transfer to another depot or the golden handshake was offered, and John Twitchen at Exeter and Herbie Mitchell at Newton Abbot, along with many of their colleagues, took the latter. In John's case the fear of being transferred to another depot and then being made redundant again was too great. So far as Herbie was concerned, he'd done forty-odd years' service and was close to retirement anyway. He saw the run-down of Newton Abbot depot and its gradual and irrevocable decline as an important railway centre. He saw the steam depot converted to diesel repair depot and the coaling plant demolished, and with this run-down came a change in attitude

of the men towards work.

John Twitchen maintained that the deterioration in attitude and in morale began as steam traction ended, a view borne out by Herbie Mitchell. As John and I stood talking by Paignton South box, a class 45 diesel went over the crossing and John received a cheery wave from the driver. 'He took his chance,' said John, 'went off to another depot, was back in Exeter within six months and he's still there.' He went on to tell me how he spent his last few months as a fireman – a second man by then – picking up rails from closed branch lines and acting as brakeman on dead steam locos that were being sent for scrap. This must have made him reflect on the occasion when he was rostered to fire 'City of Truro' when it was out of the museum and engaged on advertising work for Westward TV.

'It was', said John, 'great to go to work. Even when I had to get up at 3 a.m., once I got there time was forgotten. Still, my favourite shift was 6 a.m.–1 p.m. in the summer.'

Herbie Mitchell was a little more guarded in his assessment.

'Yes,' he said in answer to my question, 'I enjoyed the job but it wasn't much fun going

Brian Morrison

58 (*above*). Diesel 45 120 on arrival at Paignton South with the twelve-coach 12.23 p.m. Manchester–Paignton on 2 August 1975.

59 (*left*). The preserved 'City of Truro' passes Dunstall Park station, Wolverhampton, with a Festiniog Railway special. Note the wealth of Great Western features from the signal box to the fine cast-iron 'Gentlemens'.

G. F. Bannister

to work on a Saturday afternoon when your friends were off to a football match!'

From the past, I turned to the present and I asked Stan Turner about the repetitive nature of the job.

'I wouldn't do it if it was boring,' replied Stan. 'I've been very lucky in always doing a job that I enjoyed. There's plenty of variation – the scenery, I would never get tired of that, the weather, and I've got a very good mate. Life on the footplate can be an absolute misery if driver and fireman don't get on. Jesse knows the job inside out and does himself great credit considering he hasn't been a railwayman.'

Both Dave Knowling and Chris Woodland agreed with their opposite numbers on the TSR – the job is never dull, never boring and the overall picture that emerges from my interviews is of some very contented enginemen, doing a job that they thoroughly enjoy. Relations with the management and the Board are very cordial and one gets the impression that in no way is it us and them but that both lines are run very much by a team. The management side is concerned with running a commercial enterprise that is preserving part of our heritage and at the same time providing entertainment; the men are concerned with running the enterprise as far as possible on traditional lines and preserving a way of life that they enjoy. I hasten to add that the DVR/TSR is not the only successful privately operated steam railway, nor is it the only successful former GWR branch. It is, however, typical of the genre and I chose it as representative because most of my research material has been drawn from deep in Great Western territory.

But let Ted Reed have the last word, appropriately enough as he had the first. I asked him for one outstanding memory, one recollection of his driving days. He sat back in his chair and thought about it for several seconds.

'An express passenger,' he answered eventually; 'night shift; all going well; a clear night, a full moon and a gently curving right hander; the moon reflecting from the rails and you're running with all signals clear. You can't beat it.'

T. G. FI

60. Crew change on class 52 'Western Nobleman' at Swindon, December 1976. The conversation could have been: 'Jolly sight warmer than a King today, mate.'

# Index